Peter. R. Peel. 1990.

CONRAD VOSS BARK
ON FLYFISHING

CONRAD VOSS BARK
ON FLYFISHING

UNWIN

HYMAN

London   Sydney

First published in Great Britain by the Trade Division of
Unwin Hyman Limited, 1989

Unwin Hyman Limited,
15–17 Broadwick Street, London W1V 1FP

Allen & Unwin Australia Pty Ltd
8 Napier Street, North Sydney, NSW 2060, Australia

Allen & Unwin New Zealand Pty Ltd
Compusales Building, 75 Ghuznee Street, Wellington, New Zealand

British Library Cataloguing in Publication Data
Voss Bark, Conrad, *1913–*
  Conrad Voss Bark on fly fishing.
  1. Fly fishing
  I. Title
  799.1'2
  ISBN 0–04–440407–7

Phototypeset by Computape (Pickering) Ltd, North Yorkshire
Printed in Great Britain at the University Press, Cambridge

For Anne

Also by Conrad Voss Bark

Fishing for Lake Trout
The Encyclopaedia of Fly Fishing
A Fly on the Water

CONTENTS

INTRODUCTION

In recent years angling with imitation bait has come to be accepted as fly fishing. This is a mistake. The fly rod is indeed so versatile that it can be used to fish bait of almost any kind, real or artificial, with great facility, but this is angling with a fly rod, not fishing a fly.

Fly fishing for trout, sea trout and salmon is a traditional art or craft of its own, separate and distinct from other forms of angling. The purpose of this book is to explain and explore the ways and means of fishing a fly for those who would like to follow this tradition.

CONRAD VOSS BARK
Lifton, Devon, 1988

PART ONE

THE PRELIMINARIES

A FLY IS A FLY

It was called a fly; but no fly like it ever swam in the air
or flew through water.

Henry Williamson, *Salar the Salmon*, 1946

A fly has wings. It is true that many strange creatures can be cast
with a fly rod, such as plastic shrimps and worms and woolly larvae
with wobbly legs but it is difficult to think of these as flies unless
words have lost their meaning.

I started off, like most of us, happily fishing weighted nymphs
and pupae deep down in rivers and lakes, and caught many fish with
them too, and in the days when my eyesight was better I could take
a trout from a chalk stream with a weighted Sawyer nymph and felt
very proud of myself for doing so.

I was among those who experimented at Blagdon with making
strange underwater creatures fished deep down on fast-sinking
lines, and did well with them, so that like many of my generation
because I was using a fly rod I took it for granted that this was fly
fishing. Gradually I came to realise that it was nothing to do with fly
fishing. It was fishing imitation bait.

This was really quite a startling thought and one I kept to myself
for some time for it was going against the trend of opinion with
which I felt myself surrounded. From Skues to Sawyer, from
Goddard to Walker to Lapsley to Clarke, to everyone I knew whose

writings and views I admired, and some of whom were my friends, I would become if not suspect then at least a little odd if I declared that fly fishing should be fishing a fly.

So for a long time, for many years in fact, I used imitation bait patterns less and less. Gradually the shrimps and snails and their companions disappeared from my fly boxes and were replaced by Greenwells and March Browns and other antiquities. To my surprise – and I now cannot think why I should have been surprised – they worked extremely well.

So began a long and involved process, for myself, of trying to re-establish the fly in its rightful place in fly fishing. This may seem something of a problem considering the progress that imitation bait fishing has made in the last forty or fifty years but this could be to take a superficial view. Fly fishing has the strength of a long

6

tradition behind it, admirably put by one of Cromwell's army commanders three hundred years ago when he wrote that the fish

... will sometimes take the fly much better at the top
of the water and at another time much better a little
under the superficies of the water; and in this your own
observation must be your constant and daily
instructor.*

It is sometimes said – and has been cogently argued by Skues and Sawyer and Kite and others – that a trout which is taking sub-aqueous food will not rise to the fly. This is partially true but not exclusively so. Once I began to concentrate on fishing a fly I brought up many nymphing fish to a take on the surface of the water or just below. We have, I suspect, been misled to some extent on this subject by enthusiasts and apologists for bait.

Not that there is anything to be condemned in bait fishing. It is an admirable form of angling and gives an enormous amount of pleasure to many millions of people; it is simply that for me to fish a fly is far more intellectually stimulating, more delicate, more diffi-cult, and therefore much more rewarding. It is – as an American, Robert Traver, once wrote – the most civilised way of taking a trout. That also applies to salmon.

It is difficult to say why it is so much more pleasurable than bait. There are many aspects one can explore. It begins, I suppose, with the actual creation of an artificial fly, especially if one dresses the fly oneself. Here you are not necessarily making a copy, a model, of any individual insect, but are relying partly on your imagination to create a creature which by the alchemy of light and shade and colour will present to the fish an image of life, or you may be creating purely an attractor pattern which will stimulate a predator instinct, or some other reaction, of fish such as salmon which are not interested in food.

You are in a sense a conjuror, an illusionist, not only in designing

* Robert Venables, *The Experienced Angler* (London, 1662;
Antrobus Press, 1969).

the fly but in its presentation to the fish. It is said, perhaps with some truth, that presentation is far more important in stimulating a take than the pattern of the fly. Perhaps so but it seems to me that the two are to some extent indivisible, a partnership, in which one cannot be effective without the other. Here there are further qualities to be taken into account: perception of the ways of fish, the flows and curls and patterns of water which will alter or even defeat your presentation of the fly, the muscular control and skill that is needed – together with a great deal of luck – in putting a fly precisely within a matter of inches in the exact and perfect place that it needs to be if success is likely to be achieved.

In all these things it must be remembered that the fly is for the lighter parts of the water, the surface or the upper layers, and that the middle and lower must be reserved for bait. Fly has a separate province and must not be a trespasser. A weighted hook or fast-sinking line and one is immediately over the border, and the border is to be observed for the pleasure of being there rather than on any ideological grounds. Avoid ideologies like the plague, and also avoid those fruitless arguments about, for example, whether a sedge fly fished underwater becomes a lure rather than a sedge, or whether hairwings are really wings or just hair. Such arguments will be as unrewarding as those of the medieval philosophers who spent long hours discussing how many angels might be able to dance on the point of a pin.

We must, I hope, be generous minded to ourselves as well as others, and especially so must we ask the courtesy of those who are addicted to bait, and imagine that bait is fly, and are incensed at the thought that it is not, or rather that there are people who think that it is not. In the following pages I have tried to set out some of the reasons why I was converted to the fly, how it may be fished, and some of the methods that can be employed. It cannot of course be comprehensive for it is merely one man's story of the change. At the same time it is, so far as I know, the first book of its kind for a generation or more which makes a clear and definite distinction between angling and fly fishing and tries to uphold and develop a tradition which goes back a thousand years.

THE TACKLE SHOP

The pleasures of fishing are chiefly to be found in
rivers, lakes and tackle shops and, of the three, the last
are the least affected by the weather.

Arthur Ransome, *Rod and Line*, 1929

In buying your flies or fly rods you must not rely upon what the
advertisements or the catalogues tell you but go to a tackle shop
where the man behind the counter knows more about flies and fly
rods than you do but – tactful as he is – treats your opinions with
due respect.

He must be firm but not obsequious, nor too eager to impose
himself upon you. He must know when to leave you alone to
wander and inspect without interrupting with 'Can I help you?'
which often suggests that he thinks you have been wandering about
for far too long.

It is often a great advantage if he knows your name or at least
pretends to recognize you and greets you as an old acquaintance
whom he is delighted to see again.

There is of course no need for you to know his name, though it
may be satisfactory if you do. However, it is not all that important,
for he is in some ways less of an individual than a personification of
a service, a guardian of an emporium of delights which he will be
pleased to uncover.

All the same, we must not expect too much. Those who serve and stand and wait do not always have much experience of fishing with the goods that they display. They are unlikely to be given sabbaticals on the Tweed or Test for longer than an odd day at a time. Much of their knowledge of the rivers is bound to come second-hand with the consequent temptation to pass it on as their own experience. The shop is, of course, a hive of gossip, which is one of its attractions, and the tackle dealer with a fine fund of tales is more than halfway home. Even better if he offers to do things for you which you may have difficulty in doing yourself, such as putting the backing on a new reel you have just bought. That way he will become firm in your admiration and his reputation secure.

Yet I must confess that sometimes I feel the attention of the tackle dealer must be rationed. One of the great pleasures of going into the tackle shop is not having to put up with the owner or the assistant until you ask. He should be somewhere, of course, ready for you, on call, watchful, ready to leap forward when wanted, able to sense by some strange method of perception precisely the right moment to do so; otherwise, until that happens, he is preferably invisible.

Whether such a paragon exists, and indeed if he does whether he can continue to exist with all our modern methods of marketing and sales these days, is something we might bear in mind. We do not as yet have a fly fishers' supermarket but the thought is not quite so impossible as it may appear. The store would be well appointed, we would enter by a one-way griddle, pick out what we wanted from the shelves, and pay for it at the checkout. We might get accustomed to it in time but something would be lost which is worth having. Perhaps the friendly tackle dealer might survive as some kind of adviser. We might go to his consulting rooms from time to time to have his opinions on some new line or other which has just come on the market with the inevitable claim in the advertisements that it is the best fly line the world has ever seen. But we should have to pay a pretty high fee for that kind of service. At the moment we often get it free.

There is a good deal to be said – whatever the marketing consortia may be planning – for the survival of the tackle shop in more or less the same state as we have it now. It may be said to be cost-ineffective, or whatever jargon the accountants may invent, but it has virtues which it would be sad to lose. We are at least dealing with a friendly tackle dealer who is anxious to please, as well as to sell, and does not mind passing on a good opinion or a bad one about our needs. On the whole we enjoy his company as we hope it may be possible he enjoys ours. It would be sad if he were to disappear.

EQUIPMENT

Compared with his coarse or sea fishing counterparts
the trout fisherman travels lightly laden. Essential to his
purpose are a rod, a reel, a line, an artificial trout fly and
some nylon with which to connect the fly to the line.
Beyond this basic equipment there is a mass of ancillary
paraphernalia . . . which most fishermen will acquire . . .
but none of which is vital.

Peter Lapsley, *Trout From Stillwaters*, 1981

The trouble about fishing tackle these days is that there is so much
of it. Profusion in a consumer-orientated society is all very well but
it makes our choice of tackle that much more difficult than it ever
was in our fathers' time. In those days, as I remember, you had a
split-cane rod, if you could afford it, or a greenheart if you could
not, but there was no question of a choice of line to go with it.
There was just one kind, made of braided oiled silk, and that was
that.

Today you have lines of half a dozen different colours, and a
dozen or more different weights and sizes, and all are marketed as
the finest lines that have ever been made which will enable you to
cast farther, strike quicker, and land fish more effectively than with
any other. Amid all this confusion you have experts bidding you
never to use a white line because it scares the fish while others no
less eminent never use anything else.

It is the same with rods. There is always something new on the market which we are assured in the magazines and catalogues is so much better than anything which has been made before, though it may often turn out to be more or less the same if indeed sometimes not so good.

There are also our own uncertainties. For at least part of the time we are not all that sure what it is we want. The options may be clear but our minds still fluctuate in spite of that and quite a few fishermen have spent at least part of a sleepless night worrying about something or other which may well be resolved without effort the next morning. I remember becoming anxious for several weeks to the exclusion of all else because I could not decide on some problem or other about a rod, ultimately to discover, much to my surprise, that it faded into a matter of no importance with the passing of time.

However, we cannot go on shilly-shallying for ever in the hope that whatever decision we have to make will resolve itself. There are times when we may have to buy equipment in a hurry for a venture to unknown waters, a new rod perhaps, or a different line and more backing to it than the space we have on our reel. There is a hasty search of catalogues, a consultation with friends, and a good number of expensive telephone calls, and even then advice may be confusing.

It is all very well saying, as some do, that we should buy the best rod we can afford, but that is of no real help if there are at least half a dozen which could be listed as such. The problem is not in choosing between good and bad but often between two goods which have little or no difference from one another either in price or the task for which they were designed.

In recent years it has seemed to me that if we can approach such problems of equipment from a different angle, if we adopt what has been described as a lateral approach, we may find the solution a little easier to come by. We might begin by asking ourselves which rod it would be possible to do without and if that does not work we might turn the question round and ask which rod is the more likely to arouse our love and affection. We have to live with the rod for a long time, it has to help us to our triumphs, indeed it could be said to be the main partner in achieving them, for without the rod we could not cast the fly. Therefore the rod is to be loved and cherished, and if we have a glimpse of this possibility from first sight there is not much more to be said. The rod will be ours.

But there remains the all-important feel of a rod, not only when we waggle it about in a shop but when we put it to a reel and line, for that is the test. One should avoid tackle shops where this is not possible, or where they begrudge it, and we would be wise to travel many miles if we could try out the rod on a casting pond in workable conditions. Some rods may feel top-heavy with a line, some too stiff and rigid, some not stiff enough, and if we buy one that we do not feel a real affection for it will surely lead to a divorce.

There is also, ancillary to the feel of a rod, the matter of its appearance and finish. There are, for example, many rods on the market which have a sad and depressed look about them. They have been made to be sold as quickly and as cheaply as possible. They will be a bit gaudy, with a good deal of gold lettering, snake rings instead of bridge rings, poor wrappings, indifferent cork on the butt and nothing at the end of the butt to protect the cork from an impact with the ground. All such things, and no doubt others, should make you pause. When you take rods out fishing with you you want to be proud of how they look.

I have known a lake fisherman who persisted in using a most unsuitable little toothpick of a rod because he loved it and disliked the thought of using any other. He knew, as many had told him, that a longer rod would have been better for the work in hand but the functions of a rod were to him of minor importance if it meant discarding a rod that had become a friend, part of himself, a natural and irreplaceable extension of his arm.

The same attitude of mind does not only affect fly rods. By no means. The artist Robin Armstrong gives an account in one of his books of how he took one of his collection of antique fishing reels to bed with him so that he could play with it before he went to sleep. This seems to me to be the right approach. There should be no embarrassment among fly fishermen at being in love with what

others might regard as immoment toys.

Fly lines do not as a rule inspire affection. There are some which we may have had for a long time which we are glad to see again but that is about all that can be said. They are functional, mechanistic, made solely to bend the rod and deliver the fly. However, they do have the ability to create argument.

About a hundred years ago the American fly fisherman Theodore Gordon rather shocked his fellow Catskillians by saying that fishing with a black line was much better than fishing with a white. The idea surfaces about every forty years or so, the latest only a few years back, when John Goddard and Brian Clarke carried out careful experiments which showed that on the water, outside the trout's window, when the lines were reflecting the bottom, the white fly line was vastly more visible than either the green or the brown.

Did this matter? Quite a few fishermen thought it might, quite a few thought it made little or no difference, some ignored the whole thing:

> White is a very good colour for a dry-fly line. It can
> easily be seen by a fisherman but not by a trout.*

Whether or not it can be seen, I still use a white line because I find it more pleasurable to use than a dark one. That's all. Avoid orange, purple, yellow and fluorescent-tip lines for they are designed to capture fishermen. Avoid gimmicks. Avoid advertisers who make the greatest number of claims. Avoid cheap lines.

Tapers are of interest. I use a forward-taper floating white line for stillwater bank fishing for trout as it gives a little extra length if you need it. For sea trout and salmon a double-taper floating white line is fine. I have in reserve a forward-taper intermediate line for salmon for those days when the river is high and dirty.

* Dermot Wilson, *Fishing the Dry Fly* (1957; 3rd edition,
Unwin Hyman, 1987).

I find shooting heads an abomination because I hate handling backing, especially thin nylon, in my fishing hand. Sink-tips may be useful but I dislike the unpleasant feeling of the different line density when casting.

But now let us consider all the other things that we lug about with us which seem to be essential for one reason or another, which is why most fly fishermen are overloaded.

The most convenient fishing bag on the market for holding your tackle is one similar to a camera gadget bag with two or three different compartments inside and pockets at each end. It should be kept in the car, and if you take a bag to the river or the lake it will be a satchel bag for holding sandwiches, waterproof, drinks and fish.

An old jacket with plenty of pockets will do as well as a fishing

vest, also called a fishing waistcoat. These have far too many
pockets and you never know where anything is. A jacket will take a
priest, scissors, a fly box, a few spools of nylon, midge cream and
unguents for making flies float, or drying flies, or making them sink.
As well as all that, an old handkerchief or rag, your fishing permit
and licence, and a pocket knife with such things as a bottle opener,
a corkscrew, and so on.

In one fishing book now on the market you are urged to take
toilet paper. How disgusting to leave used toilet paper on the river
bank. If you have to go, use a dockleaf or great handfuls of grass
and cover the remains.

That's enough about that.

Your waterproofs should be waterproof. The best waxed jackets
will let in water along the seams quite easily after a few months' use.

They need reproofing at least once a season. Buy a jacket with an attached hood. It is easier to use.

Plastic coats are waterproof but condensation collects inside. They can be worn over a waxed jacket. The new coats with microporous film inside two layers of cloth are waterproof, do not need reproofing, but leak if the outer cloth is pierced by thorns.

Whatever you wear, sooner or later damp will get in.

A couple of points about waders. Stocking-type waders are more comfortable to wear for long distance walking, but are a nuisance to put on and take off. Chest waders with attached boots are preferable. Whatever wader you use, try and have two things on the soles, such as diamond studs as well as cleats, or flat studs with felt, rather than having a sole of only one material throughout.

Waders are better now than they were:

> The best way to dry waders is to fill the legs and feet of
> the boots, stockings, or trousers with warm bran, oats,
> or barley, which should be shaken out as soon as it
> begins to cool.*

* H. Cholmondely Pennell, *Fishing* (The Badminton Library, 1893).

SETTING OUT

Escaping to the Stone Age by the morning train from
Manchester, the fisherman engages in an activity that
allows him to shed the centuries as a dog shakes off
water and to recapture not his own youth merely but the
youth of the world.

Arthur Ransome, *Rod and Line*, 1929

Part of the pleasure of going fishing lies in the preparation – the
pleasure of opening cupboards, taking out rods, cleaning and
repairing tackle, filling the empty places in the fly box, buying or
making up new leaders, and a hundred other preoccupations that
lead to a growing excitement of anticipation.

Before we go, we have to assuage our feeling of guilt, if we
suffer such sensitivities, at leaving work at lunch time on Thursday,
and not returning until rather late on Monday morning, or whatever the arrangements may be. A bribe of some kind – perhaps the
promise of a trout if we feel we are able to carry it out – or an appeal
to the better nature of our colleagues to give us time off to recover
from all the anxieties of work we have been enduring may be
enough.

With our family we have to be pretty firm for they have suffered
all the excuses that have been trotted out over the years. Too
frequent desertions of wives can twinge the conscience but we

know from past experience that this is momentary and that our sense of guilt cannot survive the sight of a rise.

There are those who go fishing to escape from their troubles. I remember sitting on a seat by a chalk stream listening to a Harley Street specialist. He said he had tried various diversions such as sailing and golf but had found that only fly fishing concentrated his mind so much that while engaged in addressing the trout he could think of nothing but the task in hand. 'I then stop worrying', he said, 'whether I have killed my patients.'

On balance, the stresses and strains of cities slip easily from our shoulders. Preparing our escape, collecting our tackle, is a sufficient anodyne for most workaday anxieties. Should we take a landing net, will one sweater be enough? One question piles upon another until confusion and growing excitement drive all other thoughts from our heads.

To take the matter of a landing net. I suppose over the years I must have got through a good half-dozen or more. Some had handles that were too short, some too long; some were supposed to have an extending handle which did not extend when we wanted it to. They all seemed satisfactory when I bought them, as most things do, but after a time defects began to show one way or another. Trout nets were the most fickle. For salmon a gye net which has a shoulder sling seems to have lasted best, a faithful servant that goes back at least 25 years, if not more, and has taken fish up to a whisker short of twenty pounds.

So far as trout are concerned, several cast-off nets have gone to rummage sales, others to the dustbin in a sudden fit of rage, and one, I remember, was given for some reason to a boy scout group. The net I have at the moment is collapsible, with a fairly short mesh which does not hang down much below the knees. It has behaved reasonably so far but I do not bank on it.

The Americans have obviously suffered from nets as much as we have. Their solution is to have a kind of token net like a tennis racket hung from the back of the neck, where it is out of the way as well as out of reach, and to take all their fish by hand, turning them upside down to remove the hook, and replacing them in the water right way up with their head upstream until they have recovered from what must be a fairly traumatic experience.

I am not at all sure that I enjoy taking fish by hand. You grip them too tight and probably damage their livers. You also have to play them to exhaustion before you can pick them up, and, though they may be quiet enough upside down, getting them there is not quite so easy as it looks on the videos. We are here facing the perpetual dilemma of taking fish which we do not want to kill and eat. The only answer to that is not to take them.

But to come back to our other preparations for the expedition. We are unlikely to forget the rod, the tackle bag, the fishing coat or waistcoat and the waterproofs. The most likely source of trouble is the gadgets, the scissors which we took out of our coat pocket and never returned, the bottle of floatant which came unscrewed and emptied itself, things of that kind which are so enraging when we discover the loss miles away from home and the shops.

Food and drink are of the utmost importance. I must confess I am not one of the carefree debonair and open-air types who make do with a hunk of bread and cheese and a handful of fresh watercress plucked from the stream. Either the watercress is not to be found when I am there, or if there are wild watercress beds around they look unappetising and are probably polluted.

It is preferable to have home-made sandwiches, cold leg of chicken, cold sausages, Scotch eggs and in cold weather a container of hot soup. Sandwich fillings can be varied happily between Marmite and marmalade, cheese and pickle, and almost anything else that can be held between two slices of bread without dropping out. Drink should include a half-bottle of wine or a can of beer, a small amount of whisky for treating shock, and a flask of coffee ready mixed with milk and sugar, if you take sugar. The basket of food – one of those nice wickerwork ones with separate compartments – stays covered in the car. The surprising thing about picnics of this kind is that everything tastes better in the open air.

So much for the lone fisherman.

Preparing for a fishing party is quite another matter. Most of the best parties are held over several days, or nights, as the case may be.

They should be mixed – an all-male affair is inclined to be uninspiring – and one's companions must be chosen with as much care, or possibly these days with even more care, as that which should be taken by the security service checking the background of a new recruit.

Parties are best with even numbers – four, six or eight – and four is often better than six or eight. The intimate interplay of conversation is helped by a smaller number; this of course depends on who they are and on that you must be the judge. Avoid huge parties, such as the one I heard of at a fishing lodge somewhere in Wester Ross which had 25 bedrooms full of strangers.

Small parties are the best and a night fishing party for sea trout is absolutely exhilarating if the hosts live within reach of the river and old friends come to make up a foursome. You have a cold meal round about seven in the evening, make your way to the river and return some time after midnight to hot chocolate, whisky, and a hot shepherd's pie or pasties straight from the oven. After this, bed with breakfast about eleven next morning.

Another exhilarating expedition is to go miles away to a fishing lodge or hotel in the wilds of Ireland or Scotland where there is a good run of salmon or sea trout on a reasonably prolific river. You may all arrive there at the wrong time when the river is in flood but that is the advantage of being there as a party. Someone is bound to find something to do while the river roars and the rain pours even if it is only playing some ridiculous card game amid shrieks of laughter and high bidding of a penny a trick, or whatever seems appropriate. It makes up for a blank day. Sometimes it has to make up for a blank week. If you are all friends at the end of that time with your admiration for one another enhanced and your affection deepened then there is always the expedition next year to look forward to with increased enjoyment. There is more to a fishing party than catching fish.

ON SAFETY

Should you be wading [the Tweed] in February when it
may chance to freeze, pull down your stockings and
examine your legs. Should they be black or at least
purple it might perhaps be as well to get on dry land, but
if they are merely red you may continue fishing if it so
pleases you.

William Scrope, *Days and Nights of Salmon Fishing
in the Tweed*, 1843

We no longer need to wade the Tweed in February in a kilt but we
can still be very cold in thin waders. Frostbitten fingers are not
impossible. Other accidents are more likely. Do not provoke lightning by continuing to cast in a boat on a loch during a thunder-
storm. Carbon-fibre (graphite) rods are splendid conductors of
electricity. In Wales, in one year, 1987 I think it was, three men
were electrocuted by casting too near to power cables. Avoid power
cables. Even if your line does not touch them there is always the
chance of a flashover.

Such accidents are rare. Others are more common. Getting
involved with hooks the most common of all.

If your fly drops on to leaves on the opposite bank twitch it a little
and it may drop off. If it is embedded in a branch put your rod down
and pull, but not facing the fly. Your line and nylon are elastic and if

the fly pulls free it may fly straight into your face. Turn away and pull.

If your nylon is very strong, put a handkerchief round your hand before you start pulling.

Shooting men allow for wind speed. So should fishermen. Wind deflects bullets, even more a fly line. If you are casting any distance on a lake or reservoir wind pressure will move the line on both back and forward casts.

Avoid wind pressure by casting with the same hand but bringing the rod back over your other shoulder so that the fly line is being blown *away* from you.

Another way is to do a steeple cast – throw the fly line very high above your head. Another way is to cast with the other hand. Not many can.

It is easy to get a hook in your finger which goes in over the barb.

The old-fashioned way of taking a hook out was to push it through even deeper until the point and the barb were exposed, cut off the point below the barb, and then the hook can be pulled back and out. Do not try it. There is a painless way.

You need a companion with a loop of nylon or string who can be resolute and take instruction. This is the trick:

When the hook goes into the flesh it slides in and the flesh closes on the shank behind the barb. The barb is then caught in the flesh and the hook cannot be pulled out without considerable pressure and pain.

The trick is to open the channel by which the hook entered. You press down on top of the shank of the hook. This opens the

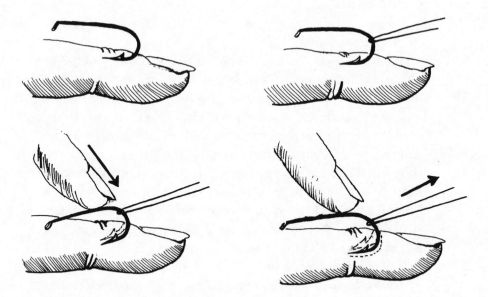

channel. Your companion with a loop round the bend of the hook can now pull the hook out painlessly providing at the moment you tell him to pull you open the channel as wide as possible.

Press down hard on the shank, shout 'Pull!' and out will come the hook with a sharp quick pull quite painlessly and without tearing the flesh.

Most ordinary trout hooks can be taken out this way. You can take a small hook out of your ear, using three hands. One hand to press, one to be pressed on, one to pull. Give the loop a quick pull, the hook comes out, the ear stays on.

Make sure that the downward pressure on the hook from point A is at its maximun as you shout 'Pull' to your companion with the loop of string, and make sure he or she knows that he has to pull sharply and at once on the word of command. This way the hook will come out painlessly.

Do not try this with salmon hooks larger than about size 8 as the barb will be too big.

To avoid all this trouble when trout fishing use barbless hooks.

Let us discuss mud.

There are various kinds. Farmyard or farmgate mud puddled by cattle is a nuisance and a bit sticky but not dangerous. Other mud can be. There are horrifying tales of the First World War battles at Passchendaele where men drowned in mud. One part of the Itchen above Winchester has chalky mud on the bank of a carrier which is like quicksand. You tread on it and down you go.

Let me tell you of another kind. You go into it just above your ankles on both feet and you stay there. The only way to get out of that kind of mud is to throw yourself on your back and pull your feet out of the boots. A companion can pull you out more easily and you will get less muddy in the process.

That's enough about mud.

Now we come to a much more serious problem which involves mainly though not entirely those who fish for salmon on those big fast Scottish rivers where the flow comes down in great white tumbling torrents over huge boulders and where you have to wade out in breast waders into a maelstrom of water.

Deep wading is dangerous.

You must use a wading staff as a third leg, making a tripod, wading out with your *back* to the flow of water, your third leg in front of you taking the strain: You do not walk. You shuffle your way out into the torrent, not lifting your feet, shuffling.

If you come to a boulder do not try and step over it. You will be completely off balance if you do. Shuffle round it upstream. Downstream of the boulder there will be a hollow gouged out by the water flow. Upstream, the water will not be so deep. Go upstream even if it means going out of your way. Shuffle at all times, feeling the way with your feet. If you keep on looking down you can get giddy. The flow of the water has a peculiar hypnotic effect.

Sometimes you may think there are easier ways of fishing.

If you feel the current lifting you then you are out too deep.

Shuffle back a bit and cast a longer line.

Avoid gravel banks. If they are on a bend of the river the gravel may have been deposited during the winter spates and is in balance, in equipoise. Additional weight on it means the gravel may slide away from under your feet.

If there is a gravel bank stretching downstream you will wade down it with no trouble but if you come into deep water, can't go any further, and have to wade back you may not be able to do so against the pressure of the current. You try hard. You turn. You lose your balance. Over you go.

Buy a buoyancy waistcoat which will keep your head above water.

There are no waders which are really safe. Felt will slip. So will studs. Plastic cleats hardly ever grip when you need them to. The safest waders are a combination of two things: cleats and tiny spikes or felt with hobs. Even those will slip. It is best to assume that all waders will slip at all times, whether you are wading on mud, on gravel, or an algae-coated rock.

If you fall into deep fast water try and get on your back and float downstream feet first. Do not try and swim. That way exhaustion lies. Paddle to the nearest bank. If the current is taking you away from the bank, go with the current. It may take you to the other bank which might mean a long walk. Never mind. Go with the current.

You may drown if you panic, wave your hands, cry for help, keep on shouting or struggling, or if you get turned head over heels in white water. Otherwise you may survive.

When you get within distance of the shore pull yourself along until you get to a flat beach. Crawl out, lie on your back, lift your legs and drain your waders. The next danger is hypothermia. Get going quickly. Find shelter and get warm.

PART TWO

THE TROUT

RIVERCRAFT

Fishing makes rivers my corrective lens; I see differently.

Nick Lyons, *Bright Rivers*, 1977

It is necessary to know a river with great intimacy, to have empathy with river life, the movement of caddis and nymph, the hatch of fly and the kind of fly, the positioning of trout, the search for food, the trouts' terror of a predator's wings. All these are a part of rivercraft, especially important if our sensitivities to the country are blunted by living too long in cities.

It is necessary to watch the river closely for some time, to be aware of the ridges of the water surface, the signs of a divergence of flow, the rocks breaking the flow, the places where trout can live without effort, held by updraughts of water, so that they keep their place with only the gentle waving of fins.

And it is above all necessary to watch for the placing of weed and weed beds, where trout feed and nuzzle among the green stems for sweet-tasting algae and plankton, the eggs of creatures and the shrimps and snails that are so easily taken from their feeding places in these underwater jungles. One must watch the gravel runs between the weed for there may be a trout there, invisible at first, only betrayed by a waving movement above the gravel that suddenly becomes a tail and the whole fish is abruptly in focus, plain and clear, whereas before there was no sign of it, though it was there.

I have too often waded upstream and seen the furrows of trout moving like lightning ahead of me, scared out of their lives by this great thumping creature approaching from behind with a great scraping and vibration of boots, waves from wading rippling upstream. If I were a cow it is as likely as not the trout would have no fear of me, but to them I am a shadow of approaching death, an alien from outer space. Trout have more knowledge of such things than we dream of.

It is the same too if we walk the bank, for then we can appear even taller and bigger and more terrifying, like a giant on a beanstalk, huge and menacing, full of strange colours and move-ments that create dread. Always try to avoid being seen even if the fish are fresh from the hatchery.

It is best to sit and watch and wait, to make an estimate of the pools and the riffles, to understand an alien condition of life, to make a map of the river in our mind before we venture into unknown territory. We stand here, we cast there, here there could be drag, over there a fish may be holed up in that pocket of water where the eddy curls, and how should it be reached if indeed there is one at such a place? Above all do not forget the overhangs of the bank, the dark places where fish like to lie out of the sun, for they have no eyelids and cannot shield their eyes against the glare. If by any chance we see a rise it is all to the good for then the trout have betrayed themselves. We know where they are.

One great fly fisher I knew would wade into a river and stand there, often as not where a riffle came out of the tail of a pool, and he would wait there for a long time, watching the water with the intensity and immobility of a heron, and he would wait until he became part of his surroundings, no more to be feared than an old fencing post or the stump of a tree; and then he would cast to precisely the right place, and if he cast once he would leave it and wait and watch before casting again. This was the great craft and technique of the hunter.

But as Nick Lyons once wrote,* the hunt is more than a hunt, for

* *Bright Rivers* (Lippincott, 1977).

the objects of the hunt are mostly to be found within ourselves, in the nature of our response and actions. It is because of this that we see differently, that the river becomes our 'corrective lens', as he called it, that we become more of a part of our surroundings, more absorbed into river life, more adjusted to a world that had previously been foreign and strange. This is the function of river-craft.

I find most pleasure in such craft by fishing a fly. It is true, of course, that there are many ways of taking a trout, by worm or maggot or imitation artificial baits, and these may often be more successful in taking deep-lying fish than a fly, but I cannot help feeling that to fish with bait, whether live or imitation, is to cross the frontier which divides the fly fisher from the angler, the bait fisher, whose territory is mid-water and the bottom of the river. The fly fisher should keep to the upper part of the water or the surface. These are his places and he should keep to them.

We should, I suggest, be a little tolerant of the occasional trespasser who in adolescent enthusiasm or a hunger for fish that is overdemanding sinks some weighted lure or nymph into the depths of a pool; but at the same time it should not be encouraged or applauded. It all too easily leads to the development of the killer. This, at one time, was nothing to be ashamed of. Indeed it was looked upon as a mark of the fisherman's skill that he took more trout than others who were fishing the same stream.

If you read the Edwardian and Victorian books on fishing you will find men boasting about their prowess in killing the greatest number of trout. At least twelve brace should be taken by any competent fisherman in the Borders. There are times when more than a hundred trout have been taken in a day from a Dartmoor stream. This is the kind of boasting that you find, and most unpleasant it all is, though it was done in ignorance and sometimes in kind-heartedness for many of the fish were given to friends and relations after such a day; all the same, it was the reason, in the belief that there was an inexhaustible supply of reinforcements, that some of our finest trout streams were fished out.

Today, with such great pressure on our rivers, we have learned, sometimes too slowly, the need to preserve our stocks of wild fish. It is by no means easy. On one stretch of the Test, so I have been told, where no more than 400 trout were taken in 1870, 4,000 were taken in 1970. Even if those figures are not entirely accurate to the nearest hundred they give an idea of what has been happening in the last fifty years or so. No river can stand that intensity of fishing without being restocked; and so we came, possibly even against our wishes, to a policy of put and take. Those who remember the wild fish of the Test grieve.

But it is not only on the chalk streams that wild fish are diminishing. It is happening on the Yorkshire rivers I fished as a boy; it is happening on rivers on the Devon moors. Pollution and the pressure of fishing take their toll, and the wildest of rivers in the most remote parts of country areas are not immune. We need, I am sure, more discipline in ourselves than we have had before. We need to curb the instincts of the hunter-killer. We need to gain the maturity which says

> ... the matter of importance is not so much how many fish are caught but rather how they are caught.*

Therefore we need to fish the fly as much as possible, in freestone and spate rivers as well as on limestone and chalk. There are times, indeed many times, in these rivers when the trout will be feeding underwater and there is little or no fly to be seen. We may be able to see trout deep down, moving from side to side, on the fin, occasionally showing the white of their lips as they take some underwater creature, an active nymph, a drifting shrimp, something of that kind. Avoid fishing the worm, the maggot, a weighted nymph or shrimp to these trout.

It is of course tempting, stimulating our killer instinct, arousing all those feelings of primitive man which we inherit, to see a good fish in position which we know can be taken by bait. Harden yourself, try not to cross the frontier which separates the fly fisher from the angler.

The American fisherman, George La Branche, a great exponent of the dry fly, described in one of his books a way of creating what he called an artificial hatch. If he found a fish feeding underwater he would cast his fly very accurately above it and let the fly drift past as far as possible directly over the fish. After the umpteenth time – he never bothered to count – the fish would rise and take.

I do not know whether I have ever consciously used La Branche's method of the artificial hatch but I used a similar technique long before I read his books. Only last season, I remember, there was a shoal of grayling and some trout, at least I thought there were some trout, on a carrier of the Test. They were all lined up in a row, taking something underwater which was coming to

* J. R. Harris, *An Angler's Entomology* (Collins, 1952).

them through a narrow gut. None was rising. All were feeding lustily on these invisible things. I do not know how long I cast to those fish, maybe half an hour, maybe an hour, though with long pauses in between to rest them, and finally quite a nice grayling came up a foot or a couple of feet through the water to the fly on the surface and took firmly as it passed.

One always remembers the failures. There was one fish on the main river at Kimbridge, a vast fish, a grandfather of a trout, which was solemnly sipping something under a willow on the far bank. It was a sixty-foot cast and the willow branches hung low over the stream so that you had to cast well above them and allow the fly to drift under the overhanging leaves. It was beautiful to try, and I tried and tried, and eventually gave it best for I think I must have had a very slight invisible drag. The fish, a nine-pounder, was taken the next day by an American on nymph.

It has sometimes been said, I think by that grand old Victorian fisherman G. E. M. Skues, that it is wrong to go on hammering a trout with a dry fly when it is feeding on underwater nymph. No one, of course, *hammers* a trout. The use of the word is emotive, and intentionally so. If you hammer a trout it will go down and stay down or scarper out of it. That is not at all the same as the dry fly passing gently overhead and Skues ought to have known it. He probably did but he was engaged in a fierce controversy with his enemy Halford at the time and was not the man to avoid giving a good blow when he could. I see nothing wrong or unethical in casting to the same trout time and again if the fish is not scared and you do not put him down. If you do, you say sorry and move on.

On the limestone, freestone and spate rivers there are many times when there are no fish to be seen, for the water may not be clear, and the surface ruffled by the current, so that you have to read the water carefully to get some idea where the trout may lie. It could be in a pocket of water, it could be under an overhang; experience and understanding and observation will be your guide. The Dartmoor streams which are full of boulders, white water and fast runs have in the past always been said to be good wet-fly water, the fly fished downstream, but I have always found the floating fly far more rewarding.

The take of a trout is always a bonus, a gift from the river god to be received humbly and with thanks. When you go to a river have in mind the trout you may take, one for yourself and maybe one for a friend, but no more. That way, by not taking too many, you will help preserve the stock of wild fish. That also is rivercraft.

THE CHALK STREAMS

Dry fly fishing is presenting to the rising fish the best
possible imitation of the insect on which he is feeding
in its natural position.

F. M. Halford, *Dry Fly Fishing in Theory and Practice*,
1889

Halford, the most eminent fly fisherman of Victorian times, was
first taught to fish the dry fly on the River Wandle, in those days a
first-class trout stream, now mainly a drain that empties into the
Thames at Wandsworth. When Halford came to fish the Test at
Stockbridge and Bossington, he had to revise his opinions about
his dry-fly patterns. They would not do. They were not close
enough imitations of the natural insects which the Test trout were
taking.

Halford was a stubborn man of independent means with a
passion for fishing. He and his friend G. S. Marryat took up their
headquarters at Bossington Mill – it is there today – and carried out
a long scientific examination of Test flies and their artificial imitations. They authorized a hundred patterns that they recom-
mended for the Test, all close imitations of natural flies, sometimes
even so close that they put in a touch of red silk at the end of the fly
to suggest its red eyes. Later, feeling no doubt that a hundred
patterns were rather too many for the average fly box, they reduced

them to thirty, or it may be thirty-three, and those were the final definitive list of the artificial flies for use on the chalk streams.

Test trout are today taken on patterns they discarded as not being sufficiently close imitations of the fly on the water. One of them was the Gold-Ribbed Hare's Ear, another was the Coach-man. These are fancy flies, not tied in imitation of any single known natural insect. Another fancy fly is the Beacon Beige, a modern dressing which suggests an unknown number of duns. Another fancy pattern, if you like to call it that for Halford would have done, is the Shadow Mayfly, a deadly fly during the mayfly season. These flies – Hare's Ear, Coachman, Beige and Shadow Mayfly – take thousands of chalk stream trout every season. It is quite possible that they would not have taken fish quite so easily from the Test in Halford's time, and indeed Halford is on record as having tried the Coachman, a favourite on the Wandle, only to find it ignored on the Test. It is not ignored today.

The reason, the only reason I can think of, is that the trout in the Test are now very different from the trout which Halford and Marryat knew in the 1870s and 1880s. The insects have not changed. We still have the same olives, the same black gnats and iron blues. It is the fish that have changed. In Halford's time they were all wild brown trout, born and bred in the river from gener-ation to generation of wild fish. From birth they had to fight for their existence, from small fingerlings onward they were brought up in wild surroundings to kill in order to survive. They were alert, and had to be, to the unknown dangers which surrounded them night and day. The mere sight of a man in the distance was enough to send them to the weed for safety.

Today there are very few wild fish in the Test or in many of the other chalk streams. The ones that are there, and in large numbers, are very different from the ones that Halford knew. They are born and bred in fish farms from farm stock and as fingerlings onwards have been used to taking their food pellets from automatic feeders. They are accustomed to the sight of man. They are taken from the fish farms at weights varying from a pound to two pounds and distributed along a strange river where they are expected to find their own food from a large insect population. They do so fairly quickly but as this is the first time in their lives they have had to rely on insect food their discrimination cannot be expected to be the same as that of fish which have been brought up from infancy to eat wild creatures and have never seen a pellet in their lives.

The number of rods in the water, the intense fishing pressure, means that in most cases today, though with some exceptions, hatchery fish may be caught within days or weeks of being placed in the river; and this, one would have thought, hardly gives them much time to learn the difference between a natural fly and a well presented artificial. This is indeed what happens. The school of close or so-called exact imitation of the natural insect, so insisted upon by Halford and his contemporaries in dealing with wild brown trout, is no longer as imperative as it was.

To say this is by no means to denigrate chalk stream fishing, for which I have an enormous affection, nor does it follow that hatchery trout are always easy to take. Sometimes they can be exceptionally difficult, especially so if there is any fault to be found in your presentation of the fly. On this I remember a wise Test keeper saying to me once that he thought presentation was 'ninety per cent of the battle'. There is also an ancillary problem about fly patterns which one is bound to take into account: the difference between the way we see our flies and the way the trout sees them.

> For many years I have used cock pheasant tail fibres for the bodies of mayflies with a red cock's hackle to repre-sent legs and wings. This has no resemblance whatever to the colouring of a mayfly as we see it, but it brings fish up far more readily than many artificials which have been dressed as seen by the human.*

The problems and the mental absorption involved in fishing the chalk streams are endlessly fascinating. To take one of so many

* Frank Sawyer, *Keeper of the Stream* (1952; new edition, Allen & Unwin, 1985).

examples: the strange behaviour of Test trout on being introduced to the Adams. This fly is very popular in America as a general pattern of floater which might suggest almost any kind of insect. It has been explained to me by American fishers as representing a caddis fly or an olive dun. The parachute dressing of the Adams is said to be deadly because the fly lies fairly low in the surface film and might – it was suggested – be taken as an emerger, a nymph transposing into a dun.

Whatever the Adams represents, when I presented the parachute Adams to trout on the Wylye and the Test last year it was taken in preference to the hatching pale wateries that were then on the water. I have no explanation. The Adams does not look in the least like a pale watery emerger, far more like a general pattern of a bug, even a beetle.

This, in a way, is the same problem that Frank Sawyer found with his red and bronze mayflies. Why on earth should these be taken by a trout during a mayfly hatch when they are so obviously different, to us at least, from the fly on the water? The simple answer is presumably this:

> There is only one secret in dry fly fishing, which is to make an artificial fly float over a trout in such a way that it looks appetising enough for him to swallow.*

This is a vast expansion of theory of the dry fly compared with Halford's time, widening the boundaries considerably from a close imitation of the natural insect to a fly which looks appetizing. Moreover, the theory seems to work well enough in practice. I have seen Dermot Wilson take fish after fish on patterns which bear no resemblance at all to our natural insects but which he makes appetizing no doubt partly by their appearance but I think mainly by the skill with which he puts them to the fish.

* Dermot Wilson, *Fishing the Dry Fly* (1957; 3rd edition, Unwin Hyman, 1987).

Then there is the new school of fly dressing, which might be called the impressionists', or even post-impressionists', for its roots go back a number of years. This creates flies with no body, only a buzz of palmered hackle from eye to bend ornamented with two hackle point wings.

The standard hackled fly is on the left, the new impressionist fly on the right. The one I know was first designed by J. Arthur Palethorpe of Hungerford Priory in Berkshire at some time in the 1950s and has been developed and marketed by one of our leading professional fly dressers, Peter Deane, who writes:

> In the hand it looks nothing like a real mayfly and it
> took me some sixteen years after I first tied it before I
> had sufficient confidence to use it myself, and what a

surprise when I did so! It is most effective and creates
an illusion or an impression of a fly, possibly because it
casts the right kind of shadow.

There is no question of matching colour. The palmered hackle is
grey cock and the two wing points are dark-red cock and bend
slightly forwards. Tying the Shadow Mayfly myself I have used
grizzle hackle wing points and dark grey points without any notice-
able difference. The last time I fished a big mayfly hatch, on the
Test at Timsbury, a lovely water, the Shadow Mayfly took every
trout with perhaps one exception, which took a Grey Wulff. There
are now other experiments involving shadow flies. The latest I have
seen is a fly used on the Wylye called a Stratford Sedge. This
follows the impressionist principle and I have no doubt others are
being designed.

All this adds to the excitement and pleasure of fishing the chalk
streams. Why should these impressionist flies be so effective? We
can have theories about them but presumably the only answer is
Dermot Wilson's: they look appetizing enough to be taken by the
trout however extraordinary and unlifelike they may appear to us.
This all adds to the fascination of dry fly, once described as being

So intriguing, so full of perplexities and uncertainties,
that the actual capture of the fish fades into
insignificance compared to the mental stimulation
involved.*

Well, yes, up to a point; certainly the mental stimulation is always
there, and so too is the appalling nerve-wracking tension as the fly
floats down over a fish and we wait, and the fly floats a little way past
the fish, and there is no move, and then abruptly the fish decides,
and comes up, slowly, deliberately, and puts its nose right under the
fly, almost touching it, and follows it downstream. Whatever

* David Jacques, *Fisherman's Fly* (A. and C. Black, 1965).

happens, whether the fish takes or turns away, the tension and the excitement stop the heart, or nearly so; certainly we cannot breathe.

Let us look at that all-important matter of the presentation of the floating fly.

First get rid of the myth that the floating fly is always fished upstream – the upstream dry fly, as they call it in the rule books and magazines. This is not so. The dry fly is certainly fished upstream most of the time but not always and not invariably. There are times when to present it properly to the fish it will have to be cast across and down.

The high priest of the dry fly, the great exponent of the method, F. M. Halford, explained how to drift your fly down to the fish:

> A considerably greater length of line than that required to cover the fish must therefore be let out when fishing a drift or a half-drift, and the action of the rod must be perceptibly checked at the forward position of the cast, so as to land the fly on the water above the fish with sufficient slack line to allow it to float down well below the fish without any drag. As before pointed out, the drift or half-drift is not usually a successful cast, and should only be adopted under conditions where it is impossible to get below and cast up to the rising trout.*

Here is an example (opposite page), at one of the carriers of the Test at Timsbury where it is impossible to cast upstream to the trout. This is one of many places where you have to use a full drift.

The trout lies well hidden under foliage. A cast from below is impossible and from directly across would only put the fly among the leaves. The only possible approach is to cast a loose line to land the fly at A and let it drift down past the trout to B, where it will be swirled out in the current to go under the bridge. This long drift

* F. M. Halford, *The Dry Fly Man's Handbook* (Routledge, 1913).

needed a very slack line. On the third or fourth drift the trout took.

Now let us go to another place where you have to cast a good deal of slack in what Halford would have called, I suppose, a half-drift. The slack is necessary in this example of a carrier of the Test at Wherwell because of the fast current, in fact you might well say a very fast current, between you and the fish (see p. 50).

The fisherman is at A and is unable to cross over to the far (left) bank. The trout is tight up against the bank and the only chance of getting it to take a fly is to drop the fly very accurately at B, where for a brief moment it will be sucked in a back eddy over the fish. The moment can only be brief because even with a good amount of slack in the line the nylon leader is going to be snatched away by the current. The trout was taken when the fly accidentally hit the bank just above B and fell down right over the fish. The trout had to be

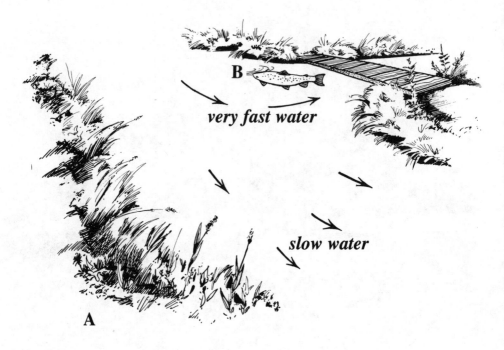

dragged out quickly towards the slow water else it would have gone down the fast current into the small carrier and under the foot-bridge into the main stream

Now another difficult cast.

The fish is on the far (right) bank and is feeding from the inflow from a carrier. It is a long cast, not far off twenty yards, and the illustration (opposite) shows a slack line cast which will allow for the line to straighten out before drag sets in. This was tried and failed. The only way that fish could be taken was a long straight cast with a straight line, dropping the fly right on the fish's nose. Drag did not matter. The fly was a sedge and the drag created the illusion of a scuttering sedge.

There are more ways of dry-fly fishing than casting the dry fly upstream.

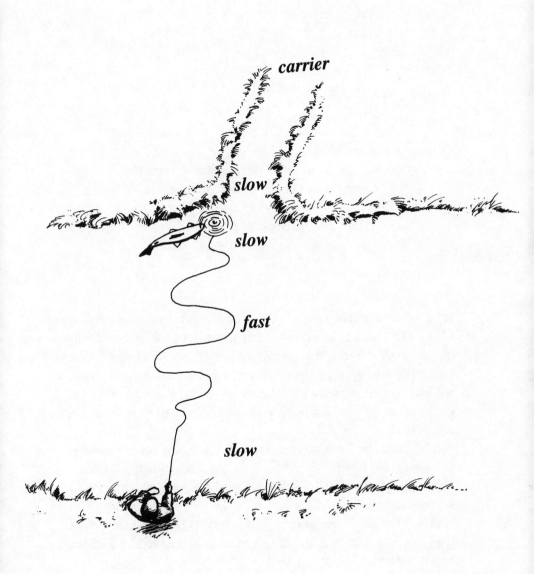

THE PURSUIT
OF PLEASURE

That a man with a small piece of split cane and a
gossamer-thin cast and an implausible artificial fly
should take educated trout in pellucid water tests
optimism and belief to their foundations.

Howard Marshall, *Reflections on a River*, 1967

Most of us, I think, possibly with some exceptions, come round
after a certain number of years of experience in fishing, especially
on the chalk streams, though not exclusively so, to a belief in the
Greek philosophy of hedonism. We may not necessarily call it that,
we may not necessarily have heard of it, but it seems to arrive
naturally as the way of a fly fisher's life and, mostly imperceptibly,
without effort.

Man, said the Greeks, pursues that which gives him pleasure,
though in the Epicurean school it is not only bodily or physical
pleasure but a simple and self-restrained life from which comes a
serene happiness which is not to be had without a measure of
regard for others. The pursuit of pleasure as the supreme aim of
man was first taught by Epicurus around 300 BC and the doctrine
seems to survive reasonably well.

We go fishing to enjoy it and we fish in the way we enjoy most,
and over the years I found that I gained more pleasure and
fascination from fishing the fly than I did from fishing bait; and this

was not so much from some doctrinal point of view, for a weighted nymph was accepted as permissible on the rivers that I fished, and weighted shrimps and snails and pupae of all kinds are allowed on the lakes, but simply and solely because I found, slowly and imperceptibly, that fishing a fly gave me more pleasure. It is true that as a boy on the Yorkshire rivers near my home I had been taught to fish the upstream wet fly, using a cast of two or three spider patterns, but in the south, in Somerset streams and lakes, I was soon converted to a weighted bait. It is a highly skilful way of taking trout and I was an addict for many years, but eventually found that there was so much more fun and fascination in the fly. Conversion, as with Paul on the Damascus road, comes suddenly, without warning, and when it does it seems the most natural thing in the world to make the change.

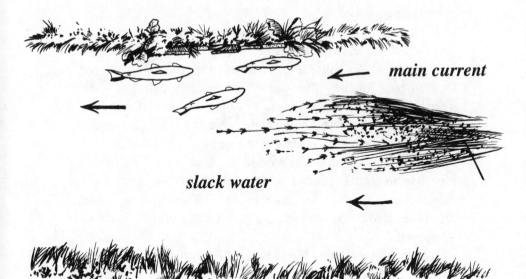

main current

slack water

A2   **A1**

But we must be careful here because there are times, indeed many times, when trout will take an underwater bait and are unlikely to rise to take a fly on the surface. Many skilled and excellent anglers like Skues and Sawyer, Goddard and Kite, have told us so and praised the induced take of the nymph. So if we switch over to a fly, an unweighted suggestion of imitation of a winged insect, do we not unduly handicap ourselves? Yes, to some extent, but not so much as we may imagine. Here is an example of a pool on the Itchen which was ideal for the nymph (see p. 53).

The river was about sixteen yards wide. A weighted nymph could be cast from A1 to the fish on the far bank. The line would snag on the thick weed. The nymph would be checked and would swing round and come up to the surface of the water. The fish were clearly visible, were on the fin, and taking something invisible that was coming down in the food stream. You could see the white of their mouths as they opened and closed. It was almost certain they were taking nymph.

If I had fished, as I knew from experience I ought to have fished, from point A1, using a Sawyer Pheasant Tail or his Grayling Bug, later renamed the Killer Bug, both weighted patterns, I was fairly sure of taking a fish. They were feeding fairly well down. They certainly were not rising to take anything on the surface. I could also have used a nymph from A2, though again I might have got my line snagged up on the fringes of the weed.

However, I had on a dry fly which I had been fishing further downstream and I was not going to bother to change. I did not expect a dry fly to take those fish which were most certainly nymphing. However, I thought I might as well try the fly to see what happened.

The trouble was drag. If you got your fly within a foot or so of the fish which were in the fast water the line lying on the slow water held back the drift and the fly dragged. In fact the drift without drag was only about two or three feet, or thereabouts. On the second or third drift the trout in the second or third position moved a little as though it was looking up towards the surface. It seemed to lift a little, to tilt up a bit. I was not certain.

I cannot now remember how often I cast. I dare say Skues would have said that these nymphing fish were being hammered with the dry fly. Maybe, but they were not scared and they went on feeding happily underwater, hammered or no. I went on casting my fly over them.

Now I discovered something that I had not seen before. The fish were lying close to the far bank and parts of that bank were supported by camp sheathing and therefore some of the wooden planks jutted out a little. It was not much, it was barely visible, but just below one of the planks the current was diverted towards me, and behind this, right up tight against the bank, was an eddy. I couldn't really see this myself but when my fly, by chance, hit the opposite bank and dropped down on to the water it was not immediately swept away by the current but bobbed in this tiny eddy. The nearest trout, either the second or the third in line, rose at once and took the fly with a savage slash. I was so surprised I struck too soon, pricked him, and he fled.

That was one example.

Now let us have a look at another. This was when my wife, Anne, was fishing a carrier of the Test at Wherwell, a most beautiful water. There was a hatchpool at one part of the beat which had a tremendous flow of water, very rough water, making a great turmoil of waves. We had been told there were some very big trout in that pool but that they would only take a nymph, and nymphing was not encouraged. This was the set-up:

It was the end of the day, we'd had a good day's fishing, and we went along to have a look at the pool before going back to the car. White water was coming through the hatch and the rest of the pool was in turmoil, and deep, so that you could not see any trout at all. We sat and looked and then Anne said she would try a big sedge, something on a size 10 hook with a good deal of hackle. She greased it well and standing at A cast across to B (see p. 56), where the current was not quite so fierce, casting to the place where there was a curl of the water. Within a very brief period, two or three casts at the most, there was a heavy take and a big struggle and eventually a brown trout of just under five pounds was netted out in the side

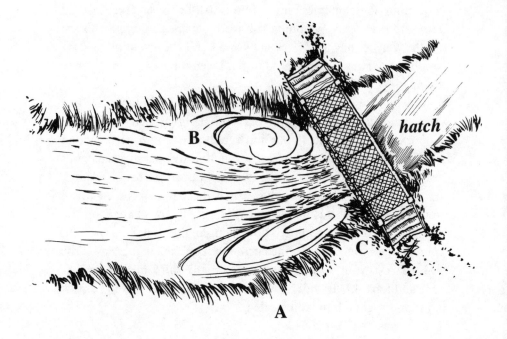

eddy at C. I have a feeling that the keeper suspected we'd taken it on a deep nymph but was too polite to say so. But we hadn't. It took the fly.

Those are two examples. There are many more.

The sedge, by the way, is extraordinarily useful in bringing up fish even when there is nothing doing and no hatch. Our fathers and grandfathers knew about this only too well:

> On days when the surface of the river is as burnished
> metal, when the thinnest gut looks like a blind-cord,
> when you reduce your flies smaller and smaller, but
> still the insolent trout disregard your almost invisible
> badger smuts and Houghton rubies; why then, reel in,
> and put on your biggest caperer.*

*J. W. Hills, *A Summer on the Test* (1924; 3rd edition, Bles, 1946).

The caperer, a sedge, can be tied on a size 10 hook but William Lunn's pattern is generally tied on a 12. It is an excellent fly and during the evening, when most of them are on the water, can be fished with a definite drag, making a wake, which brings trout up like fury. Do not underestimate the power of a dragging sedge. The natural fly takes off by a scutter over the water before it gets airborne. Scutter your caperer likewise and use strong nylon. Takes can be savage.

Part of the pleasure of the fly – and I think this is a large part of the attraction – is the wonderful variety of choice that is before you. With bait there are only about two or three patterns to use, if that, for on some streams only the Pheasant Tail Nymph is permitted and even the Killer Bug banned, so you have no real variety at all. Whereas with the fly the pleasure of choice is endless and if you tie your own flies, as you should, it becomes even more pleasurable and exciting.

One of the fascinations is that so many trout are taken on different patterns of artificial flies even during a rise to one species of the natural. I remember going round some of my friends on the Lambourn to ask what patterns they had been using during a hatch of olives. I think the fly was the large dark olive, anyway an olive, and no one was fishing the same pattern. One had on a Beacon Beige, another Kite's Imperial, a third the Pheasant Tail and as far as I remember I had on a Greenwell or maybe one of my own tyings that was rather the same as a Red Quill. Anyway, no one was using the same fly, all had good reasons for using the pattern they had on, and irrespective of pattern every one of them had taken fish.

From that you could deduce, I suppose, three things: one, that all those artificial patterns look like a dark olive, the second is that it was not the pattern that mattered but the way it was presented to the trout, and the third is that fish do not mind what they eat as long as they eat something.

These are some of the delightful speculations that are aroused by the fly, especially on the chalk or limestone streams where the water is so clear and calm and where you may often be in a position to see the fish you are trying for. The chalk streams, in particular, can have an unnerving influence on someone who is strange to them even though he may be quite experienced with the fly. I remember being taken in the early 1950s to fish the Abbotts Barton water of the Itchen, the very same stretch by Duck's Nest Spinney where the great Skues had fished for so many years. I was overawed by the occasion. I tried to cast a nymph and could not see it taken. I tried to put a dry fly over a trout in position, caught my line and fly on the reeds behind me so many times I was near to hopelessness, and ended the day miserable and fishless. Do not allow any river to dominate you in such a way as happened to me on Skues's old water. There is no pleasure in that at all.

Nor should you be afraid of the fabled chalk streams. It is all very well following the tradition and fishing an Olive when olives are on the water or an Iron Blue when iron blues are hatching and feeling yourself in the swim and doing the right thing and wouldn't Halford be proud of you, but there are times when the textbook approach does not work. When that occurs you must discard the textbook.

That, you may remember, was what happened to Skues. He started his fishing life as a follower of Halford, fishing the dry fly in the classic style. One day he was casting his fly to a fish which he saw rising but the fish refused his fly time after time. It was not a very well tied fly and on the final cast it sank. The fish took it at once.

That was an eye-opener for Skues, a short stocky little man, a London lawyer with a keen brain. He began to think about it. He examined the contents of the stomachs of the fish he caught. He assumed, rightly, that the dry fly which sank and was taken just below the surface was taken by the trout because the trout must have had the impression that this was a hatching nymph, or a nymph about to hatch, an emerger. So Skues first of all fished the wet fly, then, removing the wings, a pattern that suggested the nymph.

I quoted Waller Hills just now. He was a great disciple of Halford, a dry-fly man, a member of the Houghton Club, but time and again when spinners were on the water he would fish an Orange Partridge, a North Country pattern used in the northern way of a wet fly upstream. He would fish it in the surface film, casting to rising fish, and sometimes no doubt it would sink just a little below the surface.

It was hardly a wet fly, it was certainly not dry, so one has to compromise. It was damp.

DRY AND DAMP

'Did you catch all those trout on the dry fly?'
'No, not all, some were slightly damp.'

Horace Brown, President of the Piscatorial Society

In the days when there was fierce controversy about fishing the nymph on dry-fly water of the chalk streams, one of our oldest fishing clubs, the Piscatorial Society, resolved the conflict by permitting the use of dry flies that were slightly damp. The sophistry worked, and still works today. In practice it means you can fish an unweighted nymph – the Skues patterns – if you must but the weighted Sawyer nymphs that sink to the middle waters are not allowed. The fly is kept, as it should be, to the upper water. The society is careful to explain why:

> ...in the interests of giving all members a chance of
> the larger trout which may surface few times a season,
> and of providing conditions for an increase in number
> of these trout, the sunk or weighted nymph is not
> permitted on the Avon, Lambourn or Wylye.*

* The Piscatorial Society, *Guide to Fishing Regulations*, 1965 edition.

That has always seemed to me to be a reasonable point of view. There is no bottom scraping or middle-water angling with bugs and when the big fish come up, maybe at the mayfly, then the fly fisher has his chance.

March Brown

Blue and Black

The liberal policy of a club like the Pisces – as we all called it – paid off a thousandfold. I never remember any squabbles about dry or wet fly when I was there. No one ever thought about wet fly. We all fished dry, or we fished damp occasionally, especially with the olive spinner. I remember some excellent water they had on the Kennet at Chamberhouse where the spinner was particularly deadly even though there seemed to be no spinners on the water at the time. Two patterns did very well indeed – the Lunn's Particular and the Orange Partridge. I would fish them ungreased but with the leader greased down to about a foot above the fly. That was fishing damp. If they sank at all it was mostly just below the surface film. The Pisces were quite right. Damp and dry are pretty much the same. It goes back to the old tradition:

> Sometimes the fly are taken on the top of the water, sometimes a little under the superficies of the water.*

But why are spinners taken below the surface of the water when most of them, those we can see, fall to the surface and die after extruding their eggs? I am indebted to Roy Darlington of Abbot's Barton for the answer. He told me to look up *Baetis scambus* in Goddard. The answer was there at once. Many species of *Baetis* lay their eggs underwater.

> After this operation is completed they endeavour to surface but are sometimes too weak to break through the surface film and are trapped under it. Some, however, do break through and get carried along on the top of the film, but those that are trapped underneath it are extraordinarily difficult to see from the bank.†

Now we know why Waller Hills, a great exponent of the dry fly, one of Halford's great admirers, was so fond of fishing the Orange Partridge on the Test. A North Country wet pattern, the Partridge has a lovely orange body which turns browny-orange when wet, and speckled outstretched wings; and when it sinks just below the surface it must be a perfect image of the *Baetis* spinners. Never neglect the Orange Partridge.

* Robert Venables, *The Experienced Angler* (1662; Antrobus Press, 1969).
† John Goddard, *Trout Fly Recognition* (A. and C. Black, 1966), p. 89.

In my own experience, fishing the sunk spinner does appear helpful in persuading nymphing trout to rise to the surface. One cannot be certain of this, at least I can't, for there are so many things you suspect which are difficult or impossible to prove.

Frank Sawyer's belief about silicone-based floatants is one of them. In later years he would never use them on a dry fly because although they didn't smell to us, he believed that the trout had a far more acute sense of smell and he thought they were put off by the floatant. You can't prove that either but he was one of the finest observers of trout that we've had and his views are worth having.

Waller Hills does not tell us how he fished his Orange Partridge but I suspect it often went below the surface even on dry-fly water. There was no mention of the floatant of those days – the paraffin bottle – and I suspect he did what most of us do if we don't dunk our flies in chemicals: dry them by false casting.

For myself I don't now anoint the spinner, only most of the butt of the leader, and that seems good enough to keep the fly close to the surface.

But let me tell you of a time when I was fishing the Abbot's Barton water and had greased my fly. There is a pool there, just above Duck's Nest spinney, where two carriers come together. If you are on the right bank and the light is right – I think in the afternoon – you can see deep down into the pool, maybe four or five feet.

This time I was using a spent fly, well greased, probably a Lunn's Particular or a Sherry Spinner, and it brought up a fish right from the bottom of the pool.

I'd been trying to interest a fish in position just on the corner but had had a refusal and the fly was drifting down on the surface, circling slowly in a small eddy. I was just about to lift off and cast again when I saw a movement well down. A trout seemed to materialize out of the weed, rising very slowly in the direction of the fly. It came up very purposefully, very intently, and very delicately took the fly. It must have come up at least three or four feet.

Nymphing trout will rise to a fly.

Naturally if fly fishers persist with weighted bait the trout will take weighted bait, and so had grown the myth that a nymphing fish will not take a dry fly. It is not true.

> [I had just] reached the top of the water, a broad deep weir pool, with a rushing stream through the middle, and whirling eddies and backwaters at its head. In one of these, in a small, slow whirlpool, a big fish was lying low down, busy feeding on nymphs. I put on a Greenwell's Glory, wetted it, and after several casts managed to get it over him; he took and rushed straight down to the tail of the pool.*

If you persist with the fly, as Waller Hills did in that pool on the Kennet, you will be rewarded.

> * John Waller Hills, *A Summer on the Test* (1924; Andre Deutsch, 1985).

THE WET FLY

Fishing the sunk fly is as exciting and entrancing an art
as fishing the dry; in fact I am not sure that fishing it
upstream when you cannot see your fish is not the
highest art of all.

John Waller Hills, *A Summer on the Test*, 1924

The northern rivers, fast-flowing and bright-eyed, I knew as a boy,
but my main indoctrination many years later suffered as usual from
inexperience. I had tried spider patters, they looked very eatable,
but I had yet to meet the challenge of the Jed.

Time may have added lustre to my memory of the Jed Water on
the Scottish Borders, but I doubt it, for I saw it only last year and it
looked as splendid as ever. I first fished it thirty or more years ago
when, as a reporter, I was on my way north to a political conference
in Edinburgh. Suddenly, as I drove through the Borders, I saw the
river on my right and the sight drew me to it.

The next town was Jedburgh and I stopped outside an iron-
monger's and asked about the fishing. I was directed, surprisingly, to
the Royal Bank of Scotland, where the manager himself appeared with a large and formidable-looking book of tickets. I paid something very small for a day ticket, a shilling or so, and received some
admirable advice: to fish fine and take as many as I wanted as there
were too many fish in the stream and they wanted thinning out.

It was a lovely day, I had the whole afternoon to myself, a rod and waders were in the back of the car and some of my new spiders in the tackle bag. How happy I was as I strode across the short bright-green grass and came up over the bank and looked down to where the river ran some five or six feet below.

It was full of surprises for me. The river was as clear as a chalk stream, even clearer, but shallow, and without weed, full of scattered pebbles and little rocks over which the water chuckled and danced. Even in the pools it was a shallow stream and in parts might only have been a foot or so deep. But the surprise, the great surprise, was the fish. The pool must have been full of them for there were a dozen or more grey flashes from arrowing shadows going upstream as I came over the bank and before I took another step they had disappeared and the pool was empty.

It was like that all afternoon. I crept, I crawled, I waded, I concealed myself under bushes, there was one deep pool over-hung by branches which I felt certain was a place I might hide, but, try all my skills or what I imagined might be my skills, not a fish came to me all that afternoon. I was defeated, and a good thing too.

There are many like myself who become conceited about their prowess on a chalk stream and are therefore persuaded by their fellows and by the fishing books that chalkstream fishing is the most difficult of all, and that if you can rise a trout to dry fly in a difficult place on the Itchen or the Kennet you will be master of all you survey and that no rivers will ever hold terror for you again. The Jed taught me what nonsense that was.

The fact is that these bright little streams of the wolds and the dales, with their small wild trout, will tax anyone to the full, especially these days when there are not so many wild fish as there were. Your leader, or cast, for they still call them casts up there, should be as fine as a hair with a point and two dropper flies, mostly 16s, never bigger than size 14, and each fly as skimpy as they can be made. It does not matter a great deal which pattern you use, though each northerner has his own affections, but they must be spiders, fished upstream, and allowed to float for a little while before sinking. Do not let them stay on the water too long but lift off and cast again a yard or a yard and half beyond.

Where you cast your flies is a matter of rivercraft, of reading the water, searching for the places where a trout will be at home – under the banks, in pockets of water, sheltered by a fold in the river bed yet within easy reach of the food stream. The knowledge of the ways of water and of fish is the beginning of wisdom but the next stage is likely to be even more difficult for if we are to put our flies to a fish without the fish knowing we are there it means we have to cultivate the approach of a heron.

Watching a heron fishing is fascinating. The bird remains immobile in the shallows for a long time, then it will slowly withdraw one foot from the water, folding its toes in such a way that the foot slides out of the water without a ripple; the foot will be held immobile in the air for a while and very slowly lowered again, toes pointed, so that it enters the water a little further away with great delicacy and takes the weight of the bird without disturbing so much as a pebble. Then follows a pause, maybe thirty seconds, a minute, longer, while the bird remains completely immobile and watchful. By now you may well have become tired of waiting but if you wait a little longer the bird may decide to lift the other foot in its slow meticulous progress to the right position in the river for a strike; and the strike when it comes will be so fast you will barely see it.

That way I might have taken a fish on the Jed, for it was not my flies but my presentation which was at fault, as indeed it so often is, and I suspect that most of us or a good many of us are a little too impatient to take the necessary precautions, especially when we are approaching wild fish. It could be that we are now so used to the equable stock trout which have grown up in the company of men that we have forgotten much of our knowledge of the ways of the wilderness.

The true classic style of the northern fisherman is the short dead drift. He uses a long rod, of ten or eleven feet, and a cast of three flies, mostly spiders; walks delicately upstream casting to a rise or to likely places in the pockets of water, in the food stream, under banks, where fish may be. The flies will drift maybe a yard or so, then he lifts off, takes a step upstream, and casts again. A splendid way of fishing and – Waller Hills was right – a very tricky and difficult way of taking a fish.

But there are times when the fly needs to be drawn. I suppose this is the wet-fly equivalent of the induced take of a nymph. You find the draw useful if trout are rising and you can spot the place to cast. Drop the flies well upstream of the fish, let them come down to the fish underwater, and when they are within reach of the trout draw them towards you. I found this an admirable tactic on the Wharfe at Bolton Abbey.

There was a hatch of olives but on the Wharfe there is no drift of the fly such as you might expect on the chalk streams. They are up and away at once. But a spider drawn towards you just under the water surface is a different matter. They are taken freely.

For the flies themselves I have a fancy for the Orange Partridge, partly because I caught my first fish on it half a century ago on the Ure, partly because it is easy to tie, partly because the orange body turns a pleasing semi-brown colour when wet, and the partridge feathers suggest the veining of wings. It has taken fish for me on the Kennet and the Wylye, the Lyd and the Tamar, as well as the northern streams, and with such a record as that it has earned its place on the cast.

But, whatever flies you fancy, rivercraft must be developed with the concentration and study that comes from the habit of observation. On these northern streams the water has a myriad flows under the surface and to read the signs of what may be happening below can be a lifetime's study. I remember an old fisherman saying to me that I must practise seeing through the water. Not only must we observe the signs on the surface but we must see through an opaque surface, ignoring it, to discover what is happening underneath. The flow will give an indication of where the food stream is concentrated but in addition we must also consider how we can be out of sight of the fish and able to present the flies as if they have arrived from heaven and not from a rod and line. I hesitate to lay down rules. Rivercraft can only be absorbed by concentration on the water. But one diagram may help to give the idea.

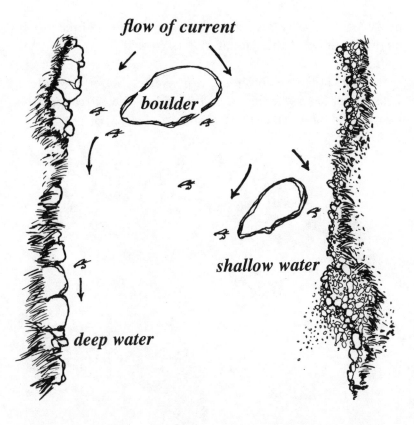

flow of current

boulder

shallow water

deep water

The places where you may find fish are marked with little flies. In all these places the water will be broken and ruffled and in the shallow parts one might expect the smaller fish while the bigger ones might well fancy the deeper water by the left bank (facing upstream) or tucked in close by the main boulder. Difficult casting, of course, and the approach must certainly be that of the heron. If not, the fish will have gone before your flies can fall.

There are times when the only way of approach with the wet fly is to fish downstream.

On the whole it is best to fish up, or up and across, for the reasons given by that great Border fisherman, W. C. Stewart, in *The Practical Angler*, first published in 1857 and reprinted many times since. The advantages are that the angler, approaching the trout from behind, is not seen by the fish, the fish is likely to be better hooked, the water is less disturbed, and the motion of the flies is more like those of the natural insect. So said Stewart, and the opinion lasts.

On some of the well bushed Devon rivers, however, the Border style cannot always be followed. Take this particular case on the Lyd, a small but prolific stream that enters the Tamar.

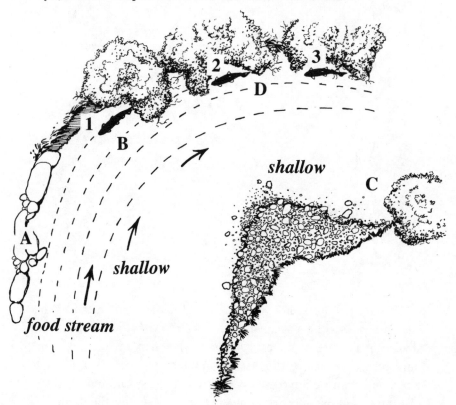

Trout number 1 should be a good one. It is where the food stream narrows, a good position, and safe under overhanging branches sheltered by tree roots. The only way you can get a fly to him is casting from A to B and letting the fly swing round in the current, then let it out a bit, and wiggle the rod top to give it life. It ought to work.

Trout number 2 is pretty well hidden but you might be able to get a fly to it by a side cast from C to D, getting the fly as far up as possible. If you can manage this and nothing happens let the fly travel well down past trout number 3. You never know. Trout number 4 might be somewhere.

The next drawing (see p. 72) is of a pool on the West Dart, another lovely Devon river with wild brown trout, high on the moors, and most exciting fishing. It is full of granite boulders and the trout live in pocket water.

The current goes in all directions round the rocks. The trout take up positions where they are sheltered from the force of the current but are in a good position to see food coming down, whereupon they will tilt their fins, flick their tails, glide out and take, and go back again.

I've marked the places where you might try to put your fly. The trout will take a wet fly, a damp fly, or a dry fly, according to your pleasure. I've put two little flies in every likely place because this is fast water and the trout may not see the fly until the second time round. It is best if you can take cover behind the projecting rock at A. On the other hand, if you are wading up you might try to take the fish at B from directly below. From A the fish is out of reach.

If you are fishing downstream on the Dart, your fly must be a wet fly for even if it is on the surface when it is cast it will be sunk by the pull of the line and the current. Sometimes it may skate a little but sooner or later it will go down a few inches or so below the surface; sometimes in swirling currents it will go deeper as the turmoil of water pulls it down.

For wet fly downstream, therefore, you will need a slightly bigger fly and on a larger and therefore heavier hook to help it sink. No weights please, no shot on the leader, no wire under the dressing, nothing of that kind. Half the life and flick and kick of a fly will be lost if it is too heavy. Heavy weights destroy the image of life which you get from the flicker of the lighter fly, or flies, in the current.

No harm in having a three-fly cast if you feel like it. If they miss one fly they may take the next. However, I find it difficult to manoeuvre more than one fly at a time on these rocky rivers and if you do get a three-fly cast in the thistles or the trees it is a devil of a job to get it out again. Play safe and use one fly.

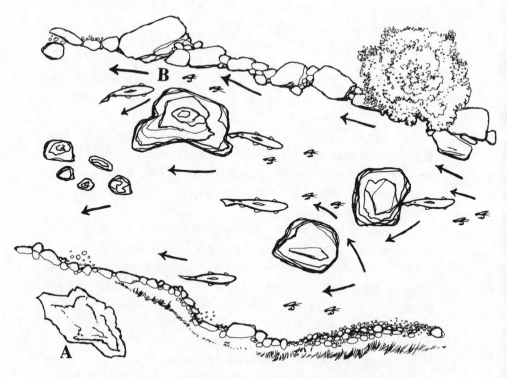

Flies for downstream wet fly should suggest a rather big insect or a small fish that can struggle against the current, providing the flow is not too fast. I find the Silver March Brown and the Butcher among the most useful patterns. There are many others, but I rather fancy that whatever pattern is chosen there should be a flash of silver about it to attract the trout's attention.

Try and guide the flies into places where it is likely that trout may take up position rather than fishing the water indiscriminately, if you can.

For example, if there is a fast gut of water in a part of the Dart which cannot be reached from below then the white water at A, opposite, is only likely to hold small trout or parr while there could be a good fish at B just where the water curls into the eddy.

This is difficult fishing. A fisherman could be at either C or D. If

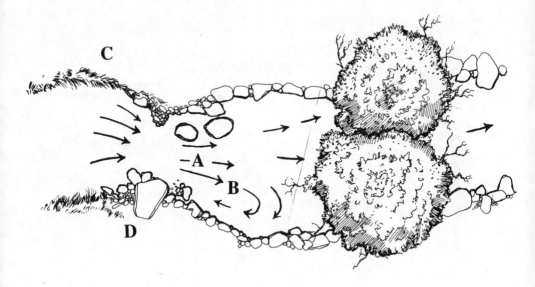

at C he has to drop his fly on the far edge of the main current in the hope it may drift into the curl of water and therefore reach the trout at B. It would be easier from D as then he can drop his fly on the curl which can then be brought round to the fish. He can also fish the eddy well down into the pool. He cannot cast from below because of the trees.

For this kind of wet fly downstream it might be a good idea to have a beetle-kind of a fly, something with a thick body, like a Coachman, or failing that the admirable Orange Partridge, which suggests a dun or spinner tumbled in the rush of water.

Do not worry too much whether you are fishing wet fly or damp fly or dry fly: in many cases the water will determine what happens to your fly irrespective of your intentions. Take this case on one of the Dartmoor rivers, the Carey.

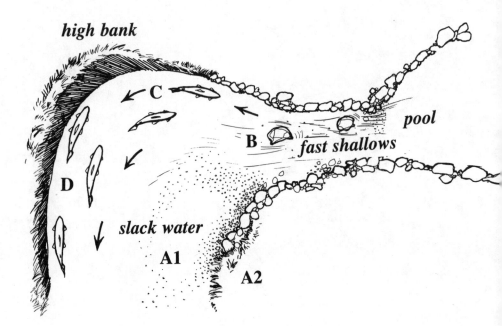

Let us suppose you are fishing upstream dry fly. You stand at either A1 or A2. You cannot go across by the high bank, nor can you cast from that side.

You suspect that fish are lying below the fast run into the pool from the shallows at the tail of the pool above. You cast your fly at B.

By the time the fly reaches the position marked C where a fish is likely to be, the fly will no longer be a dry fly. It will have been turned over and over and sucked down by the fast water.

Lift off and cast again, searching the water, and by the time you are casting the fly to reach the positions marked D it will be a dry fly again for the water surface will have been nicely smoothed out and the fly will ride it well without being sucked under.

This is what I mean by the water determining how your fly behaves.

Observation is supremely important – as much so as on the chalk streams, perhaps even more. You are not only reading the water, trying to understand where trout are likely to be, you are also watching for signs of their food. On some of the Yorkshire rivers, certainly on some of the Devon streams, there are times when there is an enormous hatch of small dark-coloured midge.

This is a time, one of several, when the trout are inclined to feed selectively. They can be very difficult to take unless you are using a fly that suggests the natural. A small Black Spider, no bigger than size 16, sometimes smaller, is the answer. If the midge are slightly bigger a Duck Fly may be the answer.

On the Ure one August there was a heavy fall of daddy-long-legs. Nothing would satisfy those fish but a Daddy fished upstream and allowed to sink. If it floated they would hit it with their tails to try and drown it. Sometimes they would try and drown it by bashing at it with their noses. As long as it was under the surface they took it properly.

Be prepared for the unexpected.

Especially so on rivers which have a good run of migratory fish as well as good stocks of brown trout. I was fishing the Lyd in Devon one summer's day with a dry fly for trout, fishing fine with a small fly, casting it under bushes on the far bank, and there was a dimple of a rise, and something went upstream like an express train. It went round one bend and then it went round another and as far as I was concerned it seemed to be heading for the spawning grounds. I had a few yards of line left on my reel when everything went slack and the fish was free. I felt he deserved it, for it was either a big sea trout or a grilse. Since then I no longer fish with a two-pound point on the Lyd. I have put it up to three.

THE LAKES

If ... the lake fisher would study the food of lake trout
and then apply this knowledge to his fishing he would
... in all probability catch more trout but what is of still
greater importance he would derive far more interest
and enjoyment from catching them.

C. F. Walker, *Lakes Flies and Their Imitation*, 1960

In the last forty years or so hundreds of new trout lakes have been
created mainly in southern England within an easy drive of London
to meet the growing demands of fly fishers. It started at the end of
World War II, when returning servicemen, looking for fishing,
found the rivers too crowded and expensive.

The small private lake has a peculiar charm that is all its own. A
stretch of water, seen through a screen of trees, small, intimate and
mysterious, draws us to its banks, we stare at the water, we look into
the depths, we wonder what monsters it hides.

Perhaps I exaggerate, maybe because as a small boy I was taken
to a pond at Newport, near Hull, where we fished for silver bream
with a scarlet-tipped float and worm on a crystal hook, and once we
hooked a real live monster, probably a carp, which was terrifyingly
strong and broke away after a fierce struggle. From then onwards I
always believed in monsters deep down in the dark of lakes.

I had the same feeling of awe and veneration for monsters when in the 1930s my father took me to fish Blagdon with a fly, or rather a team of flies, and this was about the time when Dr Bell, who had a surgery at Blagdon, was experimenting with artificial bait patterns, such as the Blagdon Buzzer – a midge pupa – and the Amber Nymph, which was not a nymph but a sedge pupa pattern.

But my real introduction to small lake fishing was in Surrey in the 1950s, and then, thanks to David Jacques, I was able to get a Sunday rod at Two Lakes in Hampshire, the pioneer trout fishery started by Alex Behrendt in 1951. Since then I suppose I must have fished a good number of small lakes – Rockbourne, Damerham, and Stafford Moor and so many others – and I was a devoted fisher of weighted imitation bait patterns.

Conversion to fly fishing came only gradually. I think the man who started it was William Nicholson, also a Sunday rod at Two Lakes, who fished nothing but the dry fly, and to my astonishment, and that of many others, caught almost as many fish as anybody else. Not that he fished hard over long hours to achieve such results. He was a very quiet, unhurried fisherman, casting a small fly in the area of rising fish, often as small as a size 16 on a very fine leader, tightening gently to a rise, taking fish of up to five pounds or more on nylon as fine as a hair. The skill, and his delight in the skill, were greatly pleasing to watch.

Two Lakes – which now has eight separate small lakes, having started from two – is what I like to think of as a civilized fishery. It is run on a subscription basis and rods go there on a fixed day a week so that everyone gets to know everyone else. It is really a fishing club and has a very pleasant atmosphere, which does not always happen on lakes, especially those open to everyone on a day-ticket basis.

Day ticket managements have trouble from time to time with what they call the cowboys, men who smuggle in a tin of maggots, take more fish than their legal limit, and sometimes fish to the sound of transistors. On a subscription fishery you can choose your rods and if anyone transgresses they are out with no refund of their subscription. Fishermen are not invariably honest and well behaved.

One advantage of the small lake fishery is that it is better stocked than the reservoirs. You pay more and there are more fish. It is as simple as that. Another great advantage is that you can reach more of the water. A good lake fishery is well landscaped and designed. There are promontories and seats, little bays sheltered by bushes, a background of pines, all giving the impression that you are in the wild, fishing a natural lake which has been there for all time.

Fishing these lakes is by no means easy. In the best fisheries the trout are not put in direct from the stock pond but are kept in a lake or a netted area of a lake for a time so that they become accustomed to foraging for themselves for insect food. It makes a difference.

Research into lake flies and methods by David Jacques over a number of years produced some interesting results. He concluded that there was no certain way of bringing a trout to a fly 'but that it is a matter of chance which fortunately we can tip in our favour a little or a great deal according to circumstances'.*

Of the most popular flies two were weighted imitation bait patterns, three were standard wet flies. The only constant factor was 'a glaring inconsistency' in the response of fish to flies. One year a pattern might be well favoured, another year practically ignored. There seemed no reason for it.

The most important element of success was 'a dogged persistence' accompanied by frequent changes of flies.

It was important not to cast too frequently and continuously in one particular area of water as this drove fish away.

Long-distance casting was, with some exceptions, less productive that casting a normal distance. Many used double-taper lines, some forward-taper.

When trout were feeding at the surface they were particular about the size and colour of the fly but not when feeding under the surface.

The use of weighted flies was now 'almost universal'.

* David Jacques, *The Development of Modern Stillwater Fishing*
(A. and C. Black, 1974).

When the dry fly was used it had to be a reasonable imitation of the fly on the water.

During the evening rise to sedge the most productive method was a running sedge, a large red palmer that created a wake across the surface of the water to imitate the scuttering of the natural fly.

With midges, a winged midge was sometimes deadly during a hatch, sometimes even more deadly than the pupa. It was fished either on or just under the surface, quite slowly, sometimes un-moving. In general the pupa was more effective.

On fishing underwater, Jacques emphasized the importance of frequent changes of fly. In my case I fished a weighted palmer nymph exclusively for several seasons without changing it at all, and my finding, which conflicted with Jacques's, was that there did not appear to be any need for a constant changing of fly patterns for underwater fishing.

Interestingly enough, there were always times on the lakes when trout seemed to 'go off their feed'. On these occasions few people took fish and fly changing was very frequent without much notice-able effect.

Yet, all of a sudden, generally when the sun was off the water towards evening, the trout would come on and this would happen on separate lakes at the same time. Most fishers would then take trout irrespective of fly pattern.

There seemed to be various rhythms of feeding which could not be predicted. The reason or reasons were not understood. One theory was that it was connected with the rise and fall of plankton, the almost invisible mass of tiny creatures such as daphnia which formed a kind of 'protein soup' in the water.

I spent some years taking air temperatures and barometric pressures to see if there was a causal connection between these and trout feeding patterns and came to the conclusion that if there was I had no real evidence one way or the other.

All this time I was entranced by the activities of our dry-fly man, William Nicholson. He would wander round the lakes looking for rising fish. As soon as he saw one he would hurry down to the nearest point on the bank and wait for the next rise. When it came he would drop his fly very quickly as near to the centre of the rings as he could get. His casting was always very fast and accurate.

If the fish did not come to his fly he would lift off almost at once and cast again and again in the area of the rise. He never cast very far or tried to cover fish which rose at a distance. His flies were mostly small duns, about size 16 or even 18, fished on very fine points of two or three pounds breaking strain. He was not infrequently broken on a big fish when it slashed at his fly.

When I was converted to the fly, I followed the same or similar tactics with patterns which might float for a moment but then sank below the surface. They were always cast to a rise or to the area of a rise. It wasn't dry-fly fishing in the Nicholson way because it was fishing a fly that sank, if it sank only a very small way below the

surface. To my surprise I found a winged midge pattern highly effective.

It is a standard pattern tied by Leonard West, Mottram and many others. There is nothing new or novel about it. It is a reasonable suggestion of a winged midge (see opposite).

The wings are light-blue hackle points, spread out a little from the body (left) and projecting down to the end of the hook (right). I mostly use dark wool with a fine silver rib for the body and a black or grizzle hackle. I have never bothered to tie green-bodied midges though I know there are large numbers of those about – the Blagdon Green Midge, for example. This may be laziness. On the other hand, I try to persuade myself that when seen from below, against the light, colour does not matter all that much. I know this will be contested.

The advantage of the hackle-point wings is in the way they support the fly as it first falls on the water. The hook and body are inclined to go through the water surface at once. If you tweak the fly once or twice the whole fly breaks through the surface and remains a little way below the surface film. It is tweaked back gently or else lifted off at once and cast again. Mostly a tweak–tweak retrieve seems best but the takes are very varied. The fly is generally quite small, a 14 or a 16 on a down-eye hook. It rarely fishes more than a foot or so below the surface.

I find this much more fascinating and interesting now than fishing a deep weighted nymph pattern. Giving up bait fishing does not seem to affect the number of trout that I take. I dare say there will be times when a sunk bait will do better than the fly but to compensate for this I have more pleasure in fishing a fly, partly because the fly is a fly, partly because it is most delicate and skilful fishing.

The big pull of a trout when it takes an underwater weighted bait pattern is indeed most exciting but I find the take of a light midge pattern either on or just below the surface even more exciting. Often it can be seen. There is a great rolling rise, or perhaps only a gentle sip, but however it is taken there is, to me at any rate, a greater thrill in bringing the trout up to take on or just below the surface than fishing deep. How you fish is a matter, ultimately, of fishing in the way that gives you the most pleasure, providing of course that you take a reasonable number of fish.

A major attack on lake trout can often be with the midge. Midges occur on every still water and if you do not want to tie your own midges there are admirable standard patterns in the Duck Fly and the Blae and Black or for that matter in the Black Spider, though I prefer a winged midge because of the way the wings will hold the fly on the surface at least for a while. Do not use floatant, though you can grease most of the cast providing you leave about a yard of tippet ungreased so that it will sink,. In effect you really grease only the butt.

The next best fly, in my experience can be the sedge.

There are some splendid standard patterns of the sedge, such as the Wickham, and no doubt the Invicta, and in Ireland you cannot do without the Green Peter, but again I like to tie my own on the same principle as the midge, with wings that will support the fly on the surface (see opposite).

The wings are dark brown, splayed out a little (left); the hackle is red or grizzle; the body can be dubbed rabbit fur ribbed with fine gold wire. A very simple pattern, size 12, 14, or 16, fished in much the same way as the midge.

These are not new patterns. Midges and sedges have been tied this way for many years but if you buy shop patterns it is important for the wings to be splayed out at the side of the body so that they will lie flat on the water and give support to the fly. They can often be pulled out to that position. As my hobby is tying flies I don't need to buy shop flies. One point to remember about the shop-bought sedge and midge – they are often too thickly dressed. If they are, snip a bit off the body or hackle and fine them down a bit until they look more like the natural insect.

Now for your secret weapons. If the flies that are fished on the surface, or just under the surface, are ignored, and midge and sedge can be ignored at times especially if there are no rises, then you must fish your fly a little deeper and for this you need the standard wet-fly design. Some fishermen may even weight them by

tying them with copper wire under the dressing. That makes them go down more quickly but I dislike weighting a fly for the heavier it is the less naturally it seems to behave in the water. A light fly, thinly dressed, which sinks well, has the advantage of responding to the slightest movement of nylon and line. A heavy fly seems sluggish. I go for the light fly every time and the pattern I put on first is either a Greenwell or a March Brown.

It is a curious thing about fly patterns. Fashions come and go and rise and fall almost as frequently as women's hemlines. The latest textbook on stillwater flies – admittedly most of them are not flies but bait – does not mention the March Brown at all, yet when I was a boy it was looked upon as a top scorer. It was first described in medieval times. The *Treatyse of Fisshynge* of 1492 advised that it should be tied with a body of 'dunne wull' with 'the wyngis of the pertryche'. It must have taken vast numbers of trout in the last five hundred years, and it is as good today as ever it was, probably better, for during that time the dressing has been polished and improved and made more sophisticated as men have worked on it.

I like also to use the Silver March Brown as a wet fly in size 16 on lakes, partly because I am carrying on a long tradition, partly because it takes trout which will hardly look at anything else. The silver body is masked and made mysterious-looking by the swept-back partridge fibres, which have a nicely speckled insect look about them. A remarkably good fly.

If the March Brown fails you can try a size 14 or 16 Butcher, a Greenwell, or a Wickham – I took my first lake trout on a Wickham, size 14 – or indeed almost any fly you like the look of. Here I think David Jacques is right. If the trout are dour then a change of fly does help and in any case a change is good for morale. It brings fresh hope.

It has occurred to me that if the hackle of a fly like the March Brown is tied as a collar – that is the hackle projects all round the body of the fly, over the wings as well – it may well give the impression of an inbuilt movement. G. E. M. Skues suggested that the buzz of hackle on a dry fly suggested the wings because the hackle looked like a blur, something diaphanous, and wings sometimes looked like that. It could be that a collar hackle seen over a body might give the impression of movement. If so, add to this the movement imparted by its passage through the water on the retrieve, and you might have quite a good impression of a lively moving insect, the inbuilt flicker of gills and legs.

Maybe so, maybe not.

It could be imagination but if you take a well tied March Brown with a good collar hackle and turn it round one way, then another, hold it to the light, see how the body glints under the hackle, how the hackle seems to change its appearance with the movement, how insect-looking it becomes, it is not all that difficult to think of it as creating an illusion of life.

Flies with a beard hackle like those you see so often on a Butcher do not have quite the same mysterious quality about them. The beard hackle, sticking out as a tuft below the body, may be easier to tie but for some reason I find difficult to explain does not have the same quality of creating an illusion.

But of course this is one of the charms of fly fishing – the study of the shapes, colours and structures of artificial flies, and the many ways in which they can be dressed to give the impression or illusion of a living creature.

And when you come to fish them you still have to think of them in the way in which they can be moved to represent a living insect. The fly is the extension of yourself, a cunning lure that is an image in your eye; you see it through the line and watch it invisible under the water, struggling to live, hackles moving, rising and falling, a puppet on a string, an image of life.

Let us now take an example of a fairly typical day's fly fishing on a small Hampshire lake at Sweatford. We arrived at ten in the morning. The lake was still, only a slight ruffle of water at the far end near the shallows, the sun already high and bright, and not a fish moving. No midge or sedge were to be seen so I put on a small March Brown, size 16. My first cast went out about ten or fifteen yards and I waited for a moment to let the fly sink, but as I waited the fly sank and something odd occurred. The take was very gentle and nothing registered on the line. The fish must have been moving at right angles to the line for quite suddenly the tip of the floating line moved slowly yet decisively to the left. I tightened but it was too late.

Nothing happened at all for the next two hours.

Meanwhile several rods using sink-tip lines and large weighted damselfly nymphs were taking fish. The trout were feeding deep and as the water was slightly coloured they certainly could not see my fly, which could only be fished a few inches below the surface. At this stage the imitation bait fishermen had all the advantage. I remained blank and was very much aware that the bait men with their big weighted nymphs fished deep were doing very well indeed.

My turn came after a picnic lunch with my friends on the bank. Suddenly the fish began to move. There were one or two rises. You could feel the difference. The fish had stopped bottom feeding and were coming up to mid-water and even fairly close to the surface. They may have been taking mayfly nymph as there were some mayfly hatching. I was uncertain. They were certainly not taking midge or sedge so I put on a small fly, a size 16 Greenwell. I had no doubt about my success this time. I was casting to feeding fish in the upper levels of water.

Why a Greenwell, and why so small?

It is easy enough to answer the last part of that question. If you use a marrow spoon and empty the contents of a trout's stomach into your hand and add a little water you will see why. A great number of insects eaten by trout are very small indeed. A 16 Greenwell is by no means the smallest. Some are no more than size 18 or 20. A trout is used to feeding on small insects and takes a size 16 fly as being just about the right size.

Why a Greenwell?

More difficult to answer. I might, of course, have been successful with a small Coachman or a Wickham. I had previously, you may remember, fished a dark fly, a March Brown. But now the trout were moving to small insects just below the surface. They might even have been large insects, the mayfly nymphs. I did not know. But it was not my purpose to fish a mayfly nymph. So I chose a much smaller artificial, a fly with sloped-back light-coloured wings, very small, which might suggest a nymph or a small bug of some kind, much smaller than a mayfly nymph. Why? I suppose the only answer I can give is that experience had taught me that a light-coloured small Greenwell would take trout providing the fish were on the feed close to the surface. So it turned out.

Within a matter of a few casts I saw a big bow-wave approaching the end of my line. I tightened into a big fish which made three or four long runs and fought deep. He weeded me and the weed lodged in a thick bunch on one of the knots of the cast about a yard or so below the line. I struggled by hand to free the nylon of weed but it was no good. The trout, pulling against the great clump of weed a few feet above him, broke free and took the fly with him.

But now there was no doubt about what the trout were wanting. In another five minutes I saw a big bow-wave coming towards my

line from quite a long distance away. This is the exciting part of fishing the fly. Your artificial is so close to the surface that almost every time you see the trout come up to the take. It was so again in this case. The wave engulfed the end of my line, I tightened, and felt the heavy weight of a good fish.

This time there was no mistake. After several heart-stopping runs I glided him in over the net. He weighed 2 lb 10 oz and my little barbless 16 Greenwell was deeply embedded in his lower lip. On the other side of his mouth was an enormous long-shank weighted damselfly nymph, size 8 or 6, which had been left there at a previous encounter with a bait fisherman.

RESERVOIR FISHING

The Welsh and the Scottish peasants are fly fishers for trout. The English artisan, through no fault of his own, has been debarred from trout fishing, and so has become the most skilful exponent of the art of bottom fishing our islands can produce. The opening of the reservoirs gave him his chance and he took it.

Ernest Phillips, *Trout in Lakes and Reservoirs*, 1914

Reservoir fishing in England began in Victorian times as bait fishing. Most of our rivers those days in the industrial north and midlands were badly polluted, some were open sewers. 'A mass of ink and stink' was how the *Sheffield Telegraph* described the River Don which drained the city and the steelworks.

In the 1860s the Sheffield Angling Club had some 20,000 members with practically nowhere to fish. The only clean water anywhere, the reservoirs which supplied the city with water, were out of bounds for fishing though they were full of small wild trout which bred in the feeder streams.

As a result of a good deal of lobbying on behalf of the anglers the city fathers opened the reservoirs for fishing. Thousands of fishermen climbed to the moors with worm and maggot and in a few years the reservoirs were fished out. From about the 1880s onwards they were restocked.

All kinds of fishing – worm, maggot, and minnow – were allowed, though groundbaiting with maggot was banned after complaints from the public that this might pollute their drinking water. So far as I have been able to discover, groundbaiting with worm was not regarded as a pollutant.

Reservoir fishing spread rapidly and became popular in many areas, at Vyrnwy in Wales, for example, and at Blagdon in Somerset, which was opened in 1904. By now some fishermen who had probably fished the fly on Scottish lochs tried the fly on reservoirs with some success. Mostly the flies were standard loch patterns used for sea trout and salmon. Some fishermen, probably very few, used dry flies such as they had fished on Lough Arrow and on the Test. They were admired though their example was not widely followed.

Ernest Phillips in 1914 summed up the general attitude:

> In reservoir fishing ... the use of the artificial fly ranks high above all other methods of angling. At the same time it is not admitted that the fly is the deadliest lure. My own experience, acquired on more than fifty reservoirs, leads to the conclusion that if angling is to be judged by results then worm fishing has no equal. We must not lose sight that the vital principle of angling ... is catching fish ... Therefore, in the matter of ethics, one form of lure is quite as legitimate as another. It does not matter whether you offer a Zulu, a real May-fly, a worm, a minnow, or a caddis grub, you are trying to deceive the fish by offering him something to eat.*

It was not anglers who wanted a fly-only rule imposed on reservoir fishing but accountants. The problem was a financial crisis. The cause was the Illingworth reel. Threadline fishing

* Ernest Phillips, *Trout in Lakes and Reservoirs* (Longman, 1914).

began to spread rapidly in the 1920s and this was a far more deadly method than anything which had gone before. More and more fish had to be stocked. The new fixed-spool reels could cast a minnow or a spoon almost halfway across even a big reservoir like Blagdon and the earlier catch limit of eight trout became much more easily taken. Whatever the fishery management did was bound to be unpopular if it meant limiting either fishing methods or the catch limits, or both, yet they could not afford to go on stocking fish in the numbers that were now necessary.

The point was not lost on the accountants that fly fishing, being a more difficult method, was less effective in taking fish than the spinner and the worm. Ultimately the accountants won. Limits were reduced on most reservoirs and restrictions on fishing methods imposed. At Blagdon, for many years a Mecca for fly fishermen, spinning was finally abolished in 1946, much to the annoyance of many of the regular fishermen there. The response of some was to design flies which took the place of the spinner. These were heavily weighted but could be cast with a fly rod, not from the reel but from loose coils of line. Regulations had to be brought in to restrict weighted minnows. Eventually the unweighted minnow-fly took its place.

Reservoir fishing has adapted well to its restrictions. The multi-coloured lure has taken the place of the spinner and can be fished at almost the same distance and depth. Imitation bait patterns have replaced the maggot and the worm.

When I first fished Blagdon as a schoolboy with my father in the 1920s it was natural that we should fish the fly even though spinning and bait were allowed. Mostly we would fish in the evenings, coming out on the afternoon bus from Bristol, sometimes going back late at night on the last bus or staying at a local inn. More often – because it was less expensive – we would fish the River Chew and my father would use the worm though I would persist with a fly, mainly, I suppose, because flies were charming to look at and less messy to handle.

Though we did not meet him we heard of the activities of one of the regulars at Blagdon, Dr Bell, the pioneer of imitation bait

fishing with a fly rod, and saw some of his creations, the Blagdon Buzzer, the Grenadier, and the Amber Nymph. My grandfather, Willie Cox, was rather contemptuous about them, saying that he saw no point in imitating maggots. Dr Bell didn't fish them all the time. At the opening of the season he would always use a spinner.

The atmosphere at Blagdon has changed a good deal since those days. The pressure on fishing is much greater. Rods can no longer be left safely in the racks in the anglers' hut ready for the next visit. Fishermen used to come to the lake by bus, on horseback or bicycle. Now there is a large car park, often full, and cars have to be kept locked. Some fishermen have also the strange habit of staking out their swims with landing nets stuck upright in the water so that one can no longer fish by walking the banks as we used to.

Nevertheless Blagdon still has a magical quality about it and I love going there. It has inspired a great deal of fine writing. I cannot resist quoting a description by Harry Plunket Greene of Blagdon from the Butcombe end at sundown:

> ...the dominant impression in my mind is the lovely colour of the evening light upon the valley as you face it looking east. It has a crimson velvet glow which hangs like an aura on the meadows and makes the shores and the scolloped hills burn with fires. It is Devonshire clay here, and the whole landscape warms pink and deepens to purple-black as the sun sinks low.
>
> And I know, too, that there was once a witch in the valley and that they drowned her when they let the water in; and one night as I grope my way home in the dark I shall stumble on Hänsel and Gretel asleep on the grass in a mist of white angels, with the myriad million stars of the Milky Way and the golden lights of Blagdon shining on their heads and winking in the watery glass at their feet.*

Lovely fairytale stuff but there is something about it which captures the spirit of the place as I remember it as a boy. I remember two examples which had the feel of magic about them at the time, and magic was the true word for it, for you had the strange feeling of being in a world which was not quite the same as a normal everyday world.

The first was when I was fishing Green Lawn, looking west to Home Bay and the anglers' hut, and as the sun began to sink behind the hill and the trees darkened, the water took on a strange look as if it was imitating a sheet of steel, absolutely metallic but with a suggestion of a furnace about it, quite flat, no ripples, but

* Harry Plunket Greene, *Where the Bright Waters Meet* (1924; Witherby, 1969).

very bright compared with the darkness of the trees behind it. The water looked odd.

Suddenly there was a kind of bubble in the metal, as if it was going on the boil, and then there was another bubble somewhere else, a little eruption, nothing big, just here and there the surface broken, ripples spreading which caught the reflection of the sunset as they fanned out. The lake, you felt, was coming alive, and my father, who was fishing near me, called out:

'Buzzer.'

In those days we had just taken up fishing Dr Bell's pattern of the Blagdon Buzzer, the big midge pupa, a simple dressing of black wool with a silver rib and a hump at the head, and there was no doubt the way the trout would take those, though I now know they would equally well have taken the Duck Fly or the Blae and Black, but I only came to an understanding of that very much later. At that time we fished the Blagdon Buzzer.

The cast was a long one, the fish were well out, and whether my father had one I do not remember, probably he did, but all I remember now was that I had a sudden heavy pull and a swirl in the water. That was all. Nothing else. I went on casting. Suddenly the rise stopped, the water changed, it was no longer like metal but ordinary dark water with a ripple on it and no fish to be seen. How is it I remember a lost fish so clearly? I do not know but it was more to do with the surroundings than the fish.

But now I will tell you of the other magical thing that took place just after sunset on the corner of Home Bay.

The Blagdon Boil is legendary and I have only seen it once though my grandfather saw it more times than that and boasted of it often on the bus taking us back to Bristol, so I had heard of it but was not prepared for it. It was either Willie Cox or Lawrie Williamson who told me the story but whoever it was it was like this:

> There are times in August when sticklebacking takes place. The sticklebacks mate in the weed and the big trout come in from the deeps and herd the sticklebacks into a corner somewhere and go through them like

savages. They're very fierce, these big trout, and the water boils with them.

I was at the corner of Home Bay, which is shallow, standing in water about up to my knees, no more, and a yard or so from the bank. You couldn't see very clearly as it was getting dark. A fish rose almost at my feet. It was a shock for it was shallow and I was casting well beyond. Then there was another rise close to the first. I could see it was a big fish from his back and the way it tore through the water. Then, suddenly, there were rises everywhere within a space of a few square yards, all round my feet, some to my side, some behind. The way the big trout rose was so savage and violent I was scared. It was like boiling water. Quite frightening in the half-dark when you weren't prepared.

I splashed out backwards onto the bank and kept on casting madly into the boil amost at my feet. I had a fish on which went all over the place, taking me well out into the backing, and by the time I was able to get the net under him the boil had stopped. Everything was absolutely calm. The turmoil couldn't have lasted more than a minute or so and then it was all over; but it was savage while it lasted and you realized that these fish were killers.

My trout weighed just under five pounds and was taken on a Silver March Brown, the fly that both Willie Cox and Lawrie Williamson said was ideal in stickleback time, right throughout the whole of August and even before for that matter. I was staying with the family at a farm nearby, Mrs Keel's I think it was, and when I got back I went to the kitchen and opened up the trout and a whole shower of sticklebacks fell out. It was solid with them, there must have been thirty or more, a silver shower falling into the sink.

There is no need to tie Polystickles or Jersey Herds to imitate minnows or sticklebacks or small fry unless you want to. A simpler dressing is the Silver March Brown. It takes just as well if not better for it has an inbuilt movement with the hackle that others lack. In smaller sizes and a nice dubbing body the standard March Brown is a fine suggestion of a water bug, but do not dress it too heavily. Give it a collar hackle which puts a kind of an aura or halo round the head. A splendid fly, it really is.

Fred Buller told me years later of the record take of fish from Blagdon on the March Brown.

In May 1905, two fishermen landed twenty trout between them, largest fish 8 lb 4 oz, average weight just over 4½ lb, total weight 90½ lb. The fishermen were M. R. L. White and R. C. Hardy Corfe and both were using the standard March Brown.

A superb general pattern which is also good in stickleback time is the Butcher and there is no need to fish it too big, a size 12 is about right; and then when the sedges are coming off in the evening you can hardly do better than an Invicta or a Wickham. I never know what to use in a Caenis hatch for there seem to be billions of these little white-bodied insects on the water and an imitation amid that crowd would be pretty hopeless. I keep on with a general pattern, something nice and visible, pulling it through the rises.

But from May onwards the pattern that I would use especially in the morning and evening would be something that suggests a midge. You can try a Black Spider, a Duck Fly or a Blae and Black, small, unweighted, nothing larger than 12, and a 14 is best. I like these flies with spread wings so that they will float a little in the surface film as if spent, and then when you twitch them on the retrieve they will sink. There are a lot of green midge on Blagdon so if you like you can use a midge pattern with a green body, quite a bright viridian green will do, and very nice semi-transparent wings, but there is no need to use a coloured midge during an evening rise. All cats are grey at night. Most midges are dark.

If no natural flies are coming off the water, if there are no rises, no sign of fish in all the vast expanse of the lake, then you must do the best you can with the sunk fly. Put on a fairly large Silver March Brown, size 12 maybe, or even 10, and fish it with a long leader and a floating line. The leader may be 10 or 15 feet long. Make sure it sinks. Then walk the banks.

Look out for weedbeds, sheltered bays, sunken rocks and old fence poles, anything that may harbour trout food. Start fanning out your casts, letting the fly sink, then drawing it in slowly. Do not stay too long in one place. You are searching for fish, hunting for them.

If the rules allow three flies, use flies of different sizes and colours, the heaviest fly on the point, say the size 10 Silver March Brown, a size 12 Greenwell in the middle and a size 14 Black Spider on the bob. You may try a floating fly on the bob and this will also act as a guide to a take. With a dour day and nothing moving changing the flies is good for the soul.

But watch out for things happening. Suddenly, in the shallows, if you have been moving quietly, not disturbing the water, you may see one or two sedge flies coming off the water. I remember seeing this once at Weir Wood just after it had opened for trout fishing – that would be some time in the 1950s – and the sedge were hatching in no more than a foot of water. As I watched several trout boiled at them. On went a sedge and it was taken by a trout no more than three or four feet from the bank. The butt of the leader was still on the land and the fly line was lying across a scrub of grass and reeds.

A fisherman in a boat, seeing me playing a fish, came rowing up towards me, making a huge bow wave and a great clatter of oars. That was too much. There were no more rises.

Whatever you do, keep away from the crowd. At Chew Valley Lake nearly everyone clusters in serried ranks on the bank nearest to the fishing lodge. Drive miles to get away. Leave places like that to fly rod fishermen using shooting heads. If you find a reservoir too crowded with bank fishermen take a boat to be peaceful and away from the noise.

There's a lot more about boat fishing in the chapters about salmon and sea trout and as that is more or less the same technique as fishing the drift on a reservoir for trout I'll leave you to look at the diagrams on those pages.

But first of all, do not stand up in a boat while you are fishing. For one thing it is dangerous and for another it means that the trout will see you from a greater distance away than if you are seated. You must have a drogue, a square of canvas with a hole in the centre and ropes at the corners which you hang over the side to slow your drift. If you have a boat on your own use it like this:

When you want to bring the drogue in at the end of a drift, if you

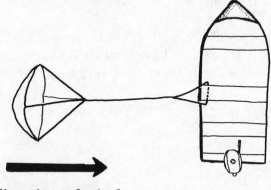

direction of wind

are sitting close to it you can pull it in without leaving your seat. Many a boat has been tipped over while the drogue or an anchor has been pulled in.

Take a cushion made up of a layer of foam with a waterproof cover. Make yourself comfortable while you sit.

Most of us know how to use an outboard motor but if not get advice from the man at the fishing lodge. Even with a motor it is good to have a pair of oars handy.

And of course you must be covered from head to foot, when needed, with waterproofs, and carry an extra sweater in a waterproof bag.

If you are in bright sun in high summer, have a cool bag with ice packs for the fish; alternatively, put the fish on the floorboards and cover them with a wet sack and make sure the sack remains wet by dipping it over the side from time to time.

Avoid putting fish into plastic bags. In hot weather in the direct rays of the sun a trout in a plastic bag can go right off colour in a very short time.

I'll talk about fly casting on the drift in later chapters but I'll remind myself now what my father told me on our first drift at Blagdon.

'Just cast in front of you, son, and when the flies land on the water lift your rod a little and just stroke the water with them. That's all. Stroke the water. That'll bring the fish up.'

PART THREE

SALMON AND SEA TROUT

SALMON IN RIVERS

And you are to observe that he [the salmon] is very seldom observed to bite at a minnow, yet sometimes he will, and not usually at a fly; but more usually at a lob or garden worm ...

Izaak Walton, *The Compleat Angler*, 1653

A worm is not to be used in salmon fishing. This is not a matter of whether it is sporting or not sporting to fish the worm or whether the worm is more efficient in taking a salmon than a spinner or a fly; it is a matter of good taste. This is not necessarily something that one is born with though perhaps more perceptive minds may acquire it before others. Even so, good taste rarely comes entirely by chance and it takes some splendid spur or some unusual event that will set one on the way to acquire it.

There are many able fishermen who have no taste at all, or very little, and probably from their character and upbringing are unlikely to acquire it. They are unaware of their defect and therefore find it incomprehensible that other people may have views which differ profoundly from their own.

Many will use poaching methods to take a fish and see nothing wrong with it providing they are not found out. Others may feel that though it may be wrong to snatch a fish with a weighted treble it is quite acceptable to take a salmon with a bunch of worms on a hook which the fish may well gorge to its stomach.

Fortunately, worming is gradually being banned on many of the major rivers and so too are other baits such as shrimp and prawn, though in some cases only for certain periods of the fishing season. Spinning with artificial minnows and spoons is still largely allowed, especially if the water is exceptionally high or turbid, otherwise fishing might not be possible at all even after travelling a long distance and paying a large amount of money for the beat.

Now we come to the fascinating question: what is a salmon fly?

It is, of course, a lure, something that will achieve a desired spontaneous or conditioned response from the fish, whatever may induce the rise and the take. Some say there is historical evidence that the salmon fly was at one time dressed with wings in imitation of a dragonfly; some say that it was dressed as a feathered lure made from a couple of red hackle feathers that did duty for a worm when the byre was frozen; and still others say the Roman legions brought it to England as they had been used to fishing the feathers for sea fish just as we fish the feathers today for mackerel off the Cornish coast.

The first designs of flies that I have seen certainly had wings. The early Victorian dressings were imaginary flies with both wings and hackle, most beautifully elaborated, small works of art, brilliantly coloured birds of paradise, fairy creatures that inhabited another world from our own. It seems to me that beauty of shape, colour and design are important factors in the salmon fly, important perhaps much more to us than to the fish, but nevertheless important.

Such flies are rarely seen in the shops these days and if they are sold anywhere are very costly, so that if you like the fully dressed salmon fly you must inevitably tie them yourself unless you are very lucky and find somewhere that still supplies them.

Today most salmon flies are tied with hair wings – you see we still use the word wing even to describe a bunch of hair – and they are just as efficient in taking fish as the fully dressed flies. But do not be deceived if some suppliers still give them the names of the fully dressed flies. A hairwing fly that someone calls a Thunder and Lightning bears no resemblance to the original feather-wing.

As to hooks, I have given up trebles because of the damage they cause. If you hook a kelt, a smolt or a brown trout on a treble it can cause severe damage to the mouth. A double causes much less damage and in small sizes is useful because it is heavier than a small single and sinks better. Such decisions are not made from the point of view of hooking power, but because flies dressed on singles and doubles seem to me more aesthetically pleasing and pleasant to use.

Avoid unpleasant ways of taking a salmon. There are many devoted wormers who still follow the method used by primitive man in taking fish. A gorge, generally a hook, was buried in meat, the fish gorged it and was pulled out with the hook in its stomach. Dead-baiters for pike and wormers for salmon still use distasteful methods of this kind. One of the latest textbooks on salmon fishing still advises that when fishing the worm the angler must wait until the hook is taken well down:

> ... however long the pause may seem, wait for the salmon to make a move. When eventually he starts to swim off and the line tightens you have only to raise the rod and make contact. By now the chances are he has the hook right back in his throat, and a fish that has taken like this will never come off.*

Fortunately many riparian owners of salmon fishing are now turning against such uncivilized behaviour. Worming is a most killing method, that is not in question, but it is not one that should be encouraged. We should devote ourselves to the uncertainty of the fly.

Edward Grey called it 'the glorious uncertainty'. This seems fair comment. The fly is an uneatable object, bearing no relationship to any known creature, designed purely to be attractive, as a Fabergé enamel is attractive, or as a witch doctor's magic charm – an

* Hugh Falkus, *Salmon Fishing, A Practical Guide* (Witherby, 1984).

incantation of feathers. Salmon-fishing textbooks do not tell you these things but that is what a salmon fly amounts to: an essay in magic.

If we adopt this point of view, and it seems to me to be the only sensible approach, then the magic must be personal to ourselves. It is we who work the magic, who work the fly, who create the illusion that it is alive and worth the time of a fish to examine; and therefore, if this argument is true, we must treat a great deal of advice given to us in salmon-fishing textbooks and magazine articles with considerable reserve. So many writers make efforts to explain what is manifestly inexplicable.

The true approach of a fly fisher to a salmon river is that he is about to become a minor magician in luring a fish to a take and that, whatever happens, all will be uncertain. This does not mean we should not make all efforts that we can to make good magic, to learn to Spey cast, to put out a reasonably long line, and so on. Not at all. In practical terms we must do our best. That is not in doubt.

What I think we must avoid is the tendency to lay down the law about how to take a fish, what to do in this pool or in this stretch of the river, or in this river compared with another, for in nine cases out of ten someone else's experience will be different and may well lead to different conclusions.

This is not, of course, to say that we should resist efforts to explain this or that or the other event according to our enquiring and curious natures, only that we should not be too dogmatic about it, for all of us suffer the tendency, often a regrettable tendency, to elevate an individual experience into a system.

To take an exmaple of the unpredictable nature of the salmon: I have only to go back to my first encounter with a very large fish on the Somerley water of the Hampshire Avon something like thirty-five or forty years ago. I was a raw untutored beginner with a double-handed rod and though I managed a trout rod well enough, when I came to the salmon rod I was very much at sixes and sevens.

I must have been trying for distance, but for whatever reason one of my first casts at the top of the beat was an absolute bird's nest. The line fell in several circles on the river and the fly wobbled after it and fell in the centre of the circles of line. Up came a very large salmon, shouldered a couple of circles of line to one side, picked out the fly from the centre, went down and hooked itself.

Never make rules from your salmon-fishing experiences. No one should construct a theory from an experience. The best advice on this that I know came from a very fine fly fisher, John Ashley-Cooper:

> A lifetime of fishing is simply not long enough to learn all there is to know about salmon fishing. There is always more to learn about methods of fishing and about the fish themselves. When a fisherman has caught some 500 salmon he is apt to think he knows the long and the short of the whole business. With 1500 fish to his rod he begins to be less certain, and by the time he has landed several thousand he has realised he will never get to the bottom of the matter. Fishing is in many ways like chess. Although there are set rules governing how the pieces move, there is no end to the subtleties of play or limits to the gambits involved. One is always learning.*

They don't tell you these things in the magazines. They should. Consider the comparison that John Ashley-Cooper makes with chess in order to explain the subtleties of play. As an occasional chess player myself, I had never thought of salmon fishing in that way before but it is perfectly true. If you look at the games of the Grand Masters the first few moves, the opening gambits, follow general principles but after that all is completely uncertain and unpredictable, and even the crucial development of an end game can bewilder onlookers as to the final result.

It may be paradoxical to say this but the advantage of the theory of uncertainty, of taking the Ashley-Cooper doctrine seriously, is

* John Ashley-Cooper, *A Salmon Fisher's Odyssey* (Witherby, 1982).

that one no longer needs to be serious. To fly fish for salmon is to
start an adventure whose outcome no one can foresee.

This is even more necessary these days because of the dearth of
salmon. In the 1960s a party on an expensive beat on Tay or Tweed
was fairly certain of geting at least one fish between them. By the
1980s certainty had gone. Pollution had increased. Runs had
declined. Even the most expensive beats had blank weeks.

For this reason it can be a miserable and depressing business to
go fishing alone. The best of salmon fishing is to be had in good
company: a mixed company too, of about four rods, all staying at
the same hotel or the same fishing lodge where good food and good
wine at dinner after a blank day can restore morale to a reasonable
level.

If you have fished all of a blank day by yourself you may have a suspicion that you have been fishing badly but if four or six rods have had the same experience then blame is to the fish or to the lack of them. Your conscience will be clear.

A party of rods will have tried various methods. Not that this means very much. In very cold weather the theory is that salmon are reluctant to rise to a fly fished on a floating line and that one should fish deep for them. In warm weather and warm water you fish a floater and a small fly. Both theories are likely to be disproved by individual rods defying theory out of indolence or indifference.

PRESENTATION
OF THE FLY

Back in the river, the salmon fasts. That is to say, it
ceases to feed purposefully. It snaps at things now and
again – if it didn't, no salmon fisher would ever catch a
fish ... Nobody knows *for sure* just why it takes a fly or
bait. Oftener than not, it doesn't.

Maurice Wiggin, *Fly Fishing*, 1958

I was brought up on the Tay to believe that there was only one way
to take a fish, a simple way, casting across the river, letting the fly
sink and swim round in the current, allowing it to dangle a little,
then a retrieve, a step or two downstream, and cast again.

That was the classic way of fishing. Then I learnt another way:
after fishing out a pool you back up and fish it again as you go,
casting square across and letting the fly swim round as you move
several paces upstream trying not to fall over the rocks. This way
the fly swims faster and provokes a take. Sometimes it did.

Out of Scotland I learned there were other ways. On the Tamar
in Devon the gillie would shout at you if you fished the classic
Scottish style, letting the fly sweep round by itself. 'Keep your left
hand moving,' he would say. 'Work the fly, give it a pull, bring it in
to you as it goes round!'

Back in Scotland that great fisherman Charles McLaren of
Altnaharra urged me always to use a dropper and dibble it over the

surface. In the magazines I read of another technique which used only one fly, cast square, and fished sink and draw. Then Hugh Falkus urged the use of a dry fly in accordance with the theories of Derek Knowles of Sutherland. These were little dolly flies that were dragged over the surface of the water, making a wake.

Finally the Irish. Peter O'Reilly and an English fisherman on an Irish river, the Eriff, taught me a splendid way to use a reservoir technique to take fish from slack-water pools. Cast a small fly upstream and strip it back fast. This is best done with a single-handed rod, as if you were on Rutland or Grafham – and very effective it is too.

So there are many ways of taking a salmon on a fly apart from the classic Scottish technique of casting across and down. You can back up, you can use a wake fly, you can do many things with the fly and all of them or most of them will take fish. On all these things too there are varied opinions, sometimes held with passionate and intense religious belief.

As for hooking a salmon, listen to what the experts tell us:

> You must strike – *Charles McLaren*
> Striking is a mistake – *H. C. Cholmondely Pennell*
> A fisherman should strike – *Lee Wulff*
> I am not fully convinced that a firm strike is always necessary –
> *Arthur Oglesby*
> Striking from the reel where it can be done is excellent fishing
> – *W. B. Currie*
> No matter what we do – fish from the reel; hold the rod high or
> down on the water; strike; pull the line with our non-casting
> hand; give the fish some slack – we will hook some of the
> fish that take and miss out on others – *Hugh Falkus*

Here, I think, Hugh Falkus is right. Whatever we do we shall hook some fish and lose others. That is all that needs to be said. In fact the best advice in practical terms was given to me by a gillie on the Spey, whose name was Hamish, whom I admired greatly for his wisdom. 'When a fish pulls you,' he would say, 'you pull him.'

So let us attempt some compromise or other that suits our nature

and does not involve taking a double-handed rod and a single-handed rod down to the river with floating lines, fast-sinking lines, shooting heads, big flies, small flies, wake flies, leaders with droppers and leaders without. That is too much like making a business of it and in any case we would need help to hump everything along.

We would do best to take local advice, and if that is not available then we ought to do some reconnaissance to find out what kind of a river it is we are going to fish. If it is a wide fast river like Tweed or Spey then there is not much doubt that the classic style will do as well as anything else and you will be able to do what W. B. Currie of Edinburgh likes to do: fish from the reel.

Having made a cast with a floating line across the water towards the far bank you hold the rod in one hand, nicely balanced along the forearm and under the elbow, keep your fingers off the line and your other hand in your pocket.

In a good stream the fly works well and if the salmon takes there is a sudden scream from the reel. Automatically, without thinking, you will respond by lifting the rod and the fish should be hooked. You can fish in the same way when backing up.

About droppers, and so on. Yes, if you want to, for a change, but it is harder work to dabble a dropper and it does mean you have to concentrate on the water.

There will be small rivers with slow-flowing water and on these the Eriff way of fishing with a single-handed rod, casting a small fly upstream and stripping it back, is highly effective, and it seems to me that if you go to a river like this a small wake fly or a small wet fly stripped back, fast or slow as the mood takes, is probably the best approach. Again, there is more work to be done, but it will be with a much lighter rod.

Small flies, doubles and singles, are the ones I use now to the exclusion of practically all others. They hook well and they fish high in the water. I find also that it is preferable to snip off the barbs so that fish we do not want to keep – kelts, smolts, small trout – can be released underwater without damage. So far I have not found that I lose any more fish by using barbless hooks than I did when I was using barbed hooks.

I have practically given up using tube flies. I have found no advantage in using small unweighted tubes compared with doubles or singles and if you use big brass tubes in heavy water it seems to me aesthetically unpleasing, not unlike using a metal spinner.

THE CHOICE OF FLY

If I have to name some of the long-established patterns I use most, I would opt for the Blue Charm, the Munro Killer, the Thunder and Lightning, Jeannie, Logie and the Stoat's Tail. But if you tell me you prefer the Jock Scott, the Durham Ranger, the Green Highlander or the Black Doctor, I should not and indeed could not offer any argument at all.

Arthur Oglesby, *Fly Fishing for Salmon and Sea Trout*, 1986

There are several hundred salmon fly patterns and each beat of a river and each gillie or boatman on a beat has his own favourite pattern for each state of the water. In my own limited experience I would say that a small double is probably the most popular fly for summer fishing and a long tube for spring and autumn for the classic Scottish style of across and down, but there may be rivers, which I have not seen, where other hooks and other methods are predominant.

But, whatever you do, take the gillie's advice on what fly to put on. Arguing with your gillie or boatman is a frustrating and self-defeating business for he knows his river better than you do. Ask his advice and take it and you will get on fine. Even when you want to change your fly it is a good idea to put the suggestion to him for

approval. If you are in a boat together and you start to lay down the law about this fly or that you will have a very uncomfortable kind of a day. A gillie is a proud man, proud of his skill and knowledge, and is to be treated as an expert, otherwise he will feel hurt. The only time you can safely disregard his option is when he is not with you.

I once carried out a minor survey of successful fellow rods and the flies they had used to take fish on the same day on the same beat of the river. They were all different in colour, shape and size, on singles, doubles and tubes.

One of our great fly fishers, John Ashley-Cooper, says there is no need to use fully dressed feathered flies as hairwings take salmon just as well.

One of our great fly dressers, Poul Jorgenson, says he is more than ever convinced that people who suggest that feather-winged flies are no longer needed are in reality covering up their inability to dress them.

I am inclined to fluctuate from one to the other.

My box has a lovely collection of single-hook salmon flies up to 1/0 with their traditional feather dressings and when I fish the Tweed I like to use a Tweed fly, a Thunder and Lightning, first dressed by Wright of Sprouston on Tweed about a century and a half ago.

At the same time for low-water fishing a Blue Charm double of about size 6 is ideal, but no doubt just as effective is a Munro or a Hairy Mary dressed with dyed squirrel hair.

Hairwing tubes are rather boring creations but powerful in taking fish, though I dislike trebles because of the damage they do if they are taken by a smolt, a kelt or a trout.

How do I choose a fly?

First of all I think it has to be visible and if the water is high and turbid you have to have something of a reasonable size and of a colour that a fish can see. If the water is low and clear then, generally, the smaller the fly the better. Those seem to be the only factors affecting your choice. The idea of a bright fly for a dull day or a bright day or a cloudy day must be among the many myths that are unproven. In general, you put on the fly you like the look of, the fly the gillie recommends, or the fly which took a fish last time you were on the water.

A cavalier approach to the choice of fly seems to me to be a moderately successful one. A great friend fishing with me on the Tweed suddenly stopped almost in mid-cast and said that he had a feeling that he had on the wrong fly. This was the time for him to change his fly, which he did, and got nothing. Even so, give way to intuition, to such superstitious feelings. Sometimes they work, sometimes they don't, but in any case you gain confidence thereby; and confidence in your fly is of supreme importance.

The best we can attempt, it seems to me, is to fish a fly we like the look of, on the principle that we must consult ourselves rather than the fish about what we are prepared to offer, and if they take all is well and if they do not all is not quite so well as it might have been.

This approach leads us into no particular heresy while at the same time it avoids any commitment except to ourselves. We do not dominate. There is no didactic formula which we want to impose on others. We are as free as anyone can be to choose a fly, for in doing so we are considering nothing more than our own set of aesthetic values. We like this fly because it is beautiful. We tie it on in the hope that it may be effective. If not we may change to another.

But the really curious thing about salmon flies is the amount of passion and argument they provoke among those who have become converts to fixed creeds about the dressings and the hooks that must be used. They are rigid and intolerant in their beliefs. I suspect it is because of their longing for conformity.

The Victorians were dab hands at conformity. They created a whole cosmology around their feathered hooks. They made rules for the unrulable, explanations for the inexplicable, reasons for the unreasonable, and all to assure themselves that they were using the right flies for the right river at the right time of day.

To do so they considered the climate, the turbidity of the water, the colour and the geology of the river bed, the size of the hook, the sharpness of the point, the relationship of the colours of the dubbing and feathers to their surrounding environment and the moods of the fish, all founded on well ascertained principles:

> Supposing the bed of the river to be of a slaty nature
> and the day dull, then dark blue, dark claret or even
> dark orange with seal's fur at the throat will form the
> best body materials. And where the fish will stand it, a
> few or more strands of peacock herl should be added
> to any built wing. Spey fish object to herl, Usk fish
> adore it ...*

It is of course a great deal of nonsense but not for the first time nor for the last has man created principles from his illusions.

* George M. Kelson, *The Salmon Fly* (1985).

The real problem is how to put the fly to the fish.

It is absurd to imagine that one can learn how to cast from a book. You need to be taught, as you would be to swing a golf club, draw a bow, climb a mountain or sail a dinghy in a howling gale.

To put a fly to a fish in a reasonable manner you need to learn more than the simple overhead, side cast and roll cast which will be adequate for trout. You will need to Spey cast as well, which is a form of roll cast involving what appears to be waving the rod in several directions at once.

Go to a good instructor and learn the Spey cast. Not all casting instructors know how to instruct, not all know how to Spey cast. I am sad and sorry that I cannot say more about Spey casting but you may be able to see a demonstration of it at one of the game fairs which are held in various places in summer and you will also find casting courses advertised in the game-fishing magazines. The best advice I can give is not to try to learn by yourself from a book as you will almost certainly become very frustrated and develop bad habits which will take time to get rid of.

I can however, help on one particular point which is nothing to do with Spey casting.

When you are using an intermediate or a sinking line with a double-handed rod and casting any distance with an overhead cast you have to draw in line a little with your free hand when you need to lift the line off the water to make a further cast. Quite a number of people draw in line with their free hand and let it drop on the water when they are wading, or even on the bank. If there are a few yards of line lying on the water or sinking under the water as you make a cast there will be a drag on the line which will prevent you shooting it to get the full distance you need. If you drop coils of line on the bank it will snag on nettles or thistles or stones and you may not be able to shoot line at all.

There is an easy way out. As you pull in line, coil it in sequence between finger and thumb on your free hand like this (opposite, above):

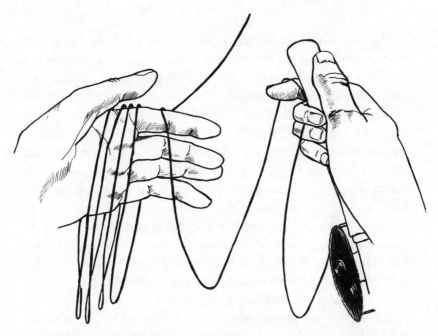

When you are ready to cast, hold your free hand on the butt of the rod with the loops of line hanging from your extended fore finger like this:

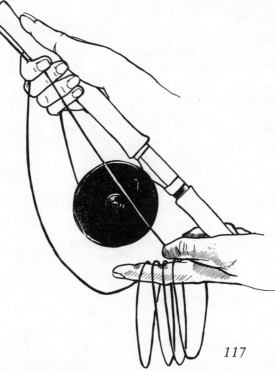

117

The butt of the rod rests in the palm of your hand, the line is held in a sequence of loops on your outstretched finger, and when you make the cast the loops should come off your finger in sequence and there will be no drag at all.

On the subject of hooks I think it is worth mentioning how difficult it is to release a small trout or a kelt which has got hooked on a salmon iron, whether a single, a double or a treble. This last season I have been experimenting with barbless hooks for salmon fishing. I have been pressing the barbs off the doubles and singles I have been fishing for salmon and sea trout.

I have taken my first salmon and my first three sea trout on hooks which have been unbarbed in this way and though the fish flung themselves about all over the river, doing several high jumps and turns, I netted them all. I have an impression that an unbarbed hook takes a deeper hold than a barbed hook. I may be wrong but I shall continue to fish barbless hooks for I am beginning to prefer them. All my trout hooks, of course, are barbless.

SEA TROUT IN RIVERS

A sea trout is a migratory brown trout; but there its like-
ness to a brown trout ends ... and sea trout fishing is
neither a branch of brown trout nor of salmon fishing; it
is a sport entirely of its own.

Hugh Falkus, *Sea Trout Fishing*, 1975

Sea trout in rivers are mostly, with some exceptions, taken at night, from dusk onwards, and I always find it surprising that the text-books rarely tell you how frightening it can be to fish a river in darkness, especially for those who have been brought up and live in towns where there are street lights and traffic and all the accus-tomed noises of habitation.

With the river in the dark you are back at once among primeval ancestors, sharing their fears of the unknown, of the ghosts of the dead, of evil spirits and unholy rites. Traces of our superstitious past are still with us and easily aroused in the darkness of the country when we are alone: a shadow that waves to us, a movement of leaves, a sighing of wind that does not sound like wind, and at once we are stricken by a leap of ancestral fear.

One foot is crossing the invisible frontier which bounds
the land of the old gods. Then comes the whistle of an
otter, the bark of a fox, and you are back in the world

119

of sentiency. Almost you fear to turn lest, black upon the moon-blanched sand, there should be the hoof marks of a goat.*

It is best to fish in company at night, two of you spread out along the river within reasonable calling distance, equipped with a torch and a whistle just in case, for you never know what may happen in the dark. You can easily trip, get caught in wire, sprain your ankle, or worse.

It is true that most sea trout in rivers are best taken from dusk onwards though they can be taken during the day, sometimes on dry fly, sometimes on wet, for I have done so on the Spey, the Yorkshire Esk, and the Devon Lyd, but on the whole it is best to start fishing when the bats come out.

There are professional fishermen who tell you of various angling ways by which sea trout may be taken, by fly-maggot, worm or spinner, but to me these are not civilized ways of fishing; moreover, they are very selfish ways as you will discover on rivers like the Border Esk or on some of the Welsh association waters where worm or fly-maggot are still permitted.

I remember the last time I fished the Border Esk. The famous Willow Pool was solid with anglers with ledgers and bubble floats fishing the worm, and a fly fisher had no chance to go through and in fact was warned to keep out of the way. On any water where coarse fishing methods are permitted the fly fisher, especially when there is a good run of fish, might just as well go elsewhere. Maybe the Border Esk will change, if it has not already done so, but before you think of going there find out if it has.

As for sea-trout tackle, you have a great choice in front of you, for sea trout can be taken on 2/0 salmon flies and size 12 trout flies on rods varying from 6 foot 9 inches to 12 feet. On some rivers traditional three-inch terrors and demons will scare fish out of their wits while on others no one seems to use anything else. The Teal,

* T. C. Kingsmill Moore, *A Man May Fish* (1960; Colin Smythe, 1979).

Blue and Silver (Hugh Falkus's Medicine) is fine on the Cumbrian Esk but is studiously ignored on the Tamar and tributaries, where thick, bushy flies are the ones to use.

I can hear you saying that it is best to take local advice and this is true, for there is no one guide to success. On the Torridge you may be advised to use flies as small as 12s, small loch flies, yet only twenty miles away on the Tamar or Lyd nothing less than about a 4 or a 6 will take fish. In other words, we are coming back to the principles of glorious uncertainty, and no bad thing, for it does allow us the liberty to fish as we please.

The curious thing about the sea trout is that, for example, a fly like a parachute fly cast across stream and dragged round to make a wake will take fish one year and will be ignored the next. I have not been able to find any consistency about this at all. This is why Hugh Falkus's book on the sea trout concentrates on a variety of methods during the night: a thin fly on a floating line, a long lure on a sinking line, a wake fly, and so on. If one of these methods does not work, another may.

I myself have got to the stage where I dislike changing tactics for it means getting out a torch, getting away from the river and tying on new flies or a new leader. I use only a floating line and keep that on for the night whether I am fishing in Scotland or in Devon. The flies are mostly of a moderate size, nothing much larger than a size 6 trout hook, a single, nothing else, and a fly with plenty of body about it such as an Invicta, a sedge, a big Silver March Brown, a Pennell, or a Bumble. In fact I fish the flies that appeal to me in the hope that with the right presentation they will appeal to the fish.

I once watched a school of sea trout rather close up to me in very clear water and I was fascinated by what appeared to be their irrational behaviour. The leading fish would idle downstream and others would follow. Then something would occur to one or other of them and they would stay there for a while as if wondering what to do, who they were, and where to go next. Then one would decide to go back upstream again, and the others would follow. They would get back to the same place but not for long. Sooner or later they would start their aimless wandering, never going all that far, always uncertain what to do next. Quite abruptly, one would lift up to the surface of the water, poke his nose through, and go down again. He was not eating. He did not know what he was doing.

On another occasion they will all hug the bottom, unmoving grey shapes, and stay there for hours with hardly a wink of a fin to show that they are alive; and if there is a movement of the gills it is imperceptible. Like the salmon they are unpredictable. Science and logic pass them by. They behave as they behave and that is all there is to it, which is why fishing for them is so fascinating.

On presentation, it may sound silly to say this but before casting to the fish we ought to know that they are there. It is not always the case. Quite a few fishers have been known to fish a pool for several hours with nothing in it. One should try to get some idea about this before starting. On some waters you can be fairly sure that certain pools hold fish but on others you can't be sure at all. Daytime reconnaissance is never wasted. If you are staying at a good fishing hotel the work will be done for you. The keeper will be out walking the banks and by evening will appear in the rod room with shining eyes and a report that such and such a pool holds dozens. Take his word for it. He wants you to catch fish.

Get down to the pool when the light is beginning to fade, and the individual leaves of the bushes on the opposite bank are becoming difficult to distinguish. If a bat is flickering about, so much the better. Do not do anything rash. Walk carefully. Make no noise. You are a hunter. If you have to wade do it now, very slowly, not making a ripple or a crunch on the stones, get out there and stay there, unmoving, still as a tree.

You are unseen, immobile, camouflaged, waiting for semi-darkness. Let some line out on the water and if it is a white line, as it should be, and becomes difficult to see then it could be nearly time to start. If in doubt do not start. You may think all this is being a little too fussy but it isn't. These fish are very shy.

Let us say that the gillie has told you, or that you know from our own reconnaissance, that the fish lie on the far side under an overhanging bush. You should have some idea how far away that is.

Strip off line from your reel, pulling off the same amount of line each time. Say you have ten pulls then you will have ten pulls' length of line on the water. Lift off and cast very very gently in the direction of the overhanging bush, making sure the line goes out straight, then keep in touch with your line as it sweeps round in the current. Pull in, say, five pulls of line and cast again, covering the same water. After a little while have eleven pulls of line on the water, then twelve, and so on.

This means that in complete darkness you still have a good idea how much line you have out on the water and how much timing it needs on the back cast. Now comes the first problem. In the dark you will almost invariably speed up your casting, giving less and less time to the line to straighten out behind. The result, especially if you are using a dropper, is a terrible tangle; or else if there is no tangle your line will drop slackly on the water with curls of line travelling down the current. If you have this slack line and a sea trout takes you are unlikely to feel it, even with your fingers on the line. Sea trout very often take a fly gently, mouthing it, so that even with a straight line between rod and fly it will feel almost as though the fly is touching a leaf. Tighten at once. Not violently. A quick flick of the rod, a controlled flick that doesn't make too much disturbance.

The curious thing is this: you can fish that part of the pool for some time, lengthening the cast occasionally, shortening it again, and even after many casts a sea trout will rise and take though it has been well covered for quite some time, maybe ten minutes, quarter of an hour, sometimes longer. The fish do not seem to be disturbed or put off by a fly dropping overhead. Maybe they take it for a natural. It is impossible to say. What will frighten them is a bad, splashy cast. They will scatter at that.

The fisher at A, if careful, can cast and cast again to the far bank, altering the distance slightly, for, although a sea trout may well ignore the first few flies that pass over him, suddenly he will respond, rise, and take. If you think your casts have been too splashy then put your flies over another part of the pool for a while just in case a fish may have strayed into the main stream before going back to the bush.

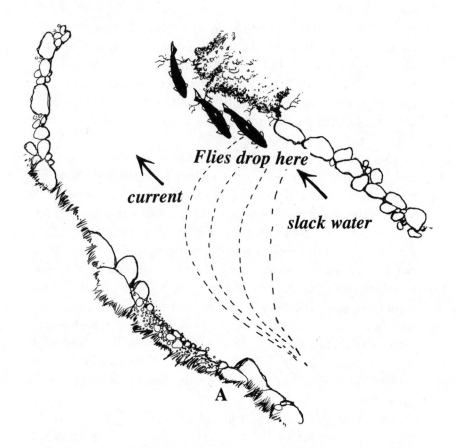

So far we have been dealing with sea trout that have been settled in the pool and taken up a position there, but it is always possible that they have left their place under the bush to move up to the shallows upstream where the water runs into the head of the pool. They may well be lying in fast tumbling water but will not necessarily stay there for very long as they want to get on upstream.

So, after trying the pool, after getting no response, make your way carefully to the run-in to the pool and fish that down. If there is a fish there and in a mood to take there will be no need to put a fly over him twice. He will take at once. If nothing happens and there is no movement, no rise, nothing happening, don't bother to wait but go down to the tail of the pool and put a fly over that. There is always a chance that the fish have been travelling upstream and have just come into the tail of the pool and are resting there for a moment.

Some fishermen I know use a dropper as well as a point fly for fishing in the dark. A splendid idea, but if you once lose your rhythm of casting, which happens easily in the dark, then you must spend a long time out of sight of the river with your torch trying to sort out the tangle. A dropper is not easy in the dark.

But there is always daylight fishing, especially in the sea pools where the fresh water meets the tide.

SEA TROUT
IN THE SEA POOL

The fish come in with the tide and are usually found in
the rough where the flowing tide meets the current of
the stream.

Charles McLaren, *The Art of Sea Trout Fishing*, 1963

Sea pools are mysterious places. I was fishing one once on Arran
Island and I had a queer sense of something odd; and though I did
not know it at the time something odd was indeed happening not a
mile away from me offshore. I was close to the unknown. I tell the
story as it came to me many years later.

Two sea fishermen were out in a boat, fishing a drift in Brodick
Bay off Arran Island where the flow of the Clyde meets the deep
Atlantic rollers. They saw a disturbance on the surface of the sea
about fifty yards away from their boat. They thought it might be a
basking shark or seals. It was neither.

The creature was longer than their boat, which would make it
over seventeen feet long. A rounded head, or what they took to be a
head, was followed by a long body. They saw no fins and the
creature moved in an up and down way with undulating movements
like a porpoise. It was no porpoise. They did not know what it was.
They watched it for several minutes before it disappeared.

After reading of a similar sighting by the naturalist Gavin
Maxwell, also on the west coast of Scotland, one of the fishermen,

Michael Prichard, plucked up courage to tell the story in print.* He emphasized that they had not been drinking, they saw this creature very clearly, and it was certainly not a creature they had ever seen before or since.

Let me tell you a story of a creature that looked very similar to the one that Prichard saw, only this time it was actually in a sea-trout pool itself, and one that I have fished myself, which is why I tell you that they are mysterious places.

This sighting was in the sea pool, or just above the sea pool, of the Newport or Black River in Co. Mayo in the west of Ireland. The story came from a man I knew well at the time and I have no reason to doubt the truth of it. He was fishing the pool just before dusk and was into a good sea trout when something large and undulating came out of the water, took the sea trout in its jaws, turned, broke his tackle as if it were cotton, made a great turmoil in the water with its long body, and disappeared in the direction of the sea.

'I had not drunk a drop before that happened,' he said, 'but I did after.'

He thought it might have been a huge conger eel but it did not look like a conger and the body was much thicker than any conger he had ever seen or heard of. If it was a sea monster then it was possibly something like a plesiosaurus, an ancient reptile with a small head, a long neck and a thick body with paddle fins. He didn't see any fins, but then he had not seen much of the body, only the long neck.

The plesiosaurus is extinct. We were told the coelacanth was extinct until they discovered one off the coast of Madagascar. However, let us keep our imaginations in check, let us not speculate too far, let us believe nothing until we see it with our own eyes and possibly not even then; even so, one does have a mysterious feeling about the vastness of the sea beyond the breaking waves by the bar of the sea pool.

Let us return to the known world, to the sea pool on Arran,

---

* Michael Prichard, *A Sporting Angler* (Collins, 1987).

where there are no monsters, only the sea trout coming in on the tide. There are breakers far out down beyond the sand bars and as the tide lifts the ripples from them come flooding in to meet the rough of the stream, jaggling the surface, obscuring the weed and the sand below.

You can use an ordinary single-handed loch-fishing rod and not too light a line if the wind is against you for you may have to put it out straight into the wind coming off the sea, and the trick here, which I'm sure you'll know, is to cut the line, as it were, under the wind close to the water surface.

I doubt if you should go less than 7 or 8 pounds breaking strain at the point, the tippet, of the leader, for there is always the chance of a salmon coming up as well. You never know. As for flies, some will fish a team of three flies, but for myself I rather fancy one will do, sometimes with a bushy kind of dropper. Patterns will be standard loch patterns though of course everyone has views about this; some will even go to the trouble of making elver flies or even catching live elvers and digging for worms or fishing a fly-maggot on a fly-spoon. Avoid horrors of this kind. They are in bad taste, uncivilized, nothing to do with fly fishing at all. All my estuary trout I've taken on ordinary loch flies, nothing much larger than a 6, the kind you would use on Hope or Beltra, Maree or Corrib, places like that.

There is a tide in the affairs of sea trout when they will take a fly in the estuary and other times when they will not, and the best time to fish seems to be an hour before high water and an hour after, but if the locals tell you it is two hours then that is fine. If you wait too long the swelling tide of the estuary will have gone home, the water will shallow, and the fish will have gone upstream.

Beware of seals.

If there is a seal near, the fish will not run or if they do run they will go hell for leather past the brackish water well upstream, scared out of their lives. You will know if there are seals around because you will see them, heads bobbing in the wave, unmistakably seals and not monsters.

Professional fishermen shoot seals but I sing to them. I remember once we were collecting mussels on rocks in a loch off the

Island of Mull – what a beautiful island that is – and I was fascinated by a whole school or covey of seals which were all over the place. We tied our boat to the rocks and the others in the party went off collecting mussels but I sat on the rock, waiting, very still, not moving at all, and the seals became curious and came in quite close making their singing noises. So I sang back to them. *Waowe waowe.* I sat on the rock and they bobbed in front of me and we sang to each other. The concert lasted for about half an hour. When my friends came back with their baskets of mussels the seals bowed and left.

Back to the fishing.

At the sea pool in Arran there were no seals and the fish were coming in with the tide, tailing over the sand bars, coming up to where the fresh water was meeting the tide, a ruffle of wavelets where the downflow of the river came against the heavy pressure of the sea. There was a huddle of a pool on the far bank, where the sand had been scoured out, which looked promising.

The water sparkled like diamonds, the sun blazed, and it seemed to me that a dark fly might be the answer at such a time, though I dare say a bright fly would have done as well. Nothing large, I thought, for it was the kind of water in which you could count the gravel and if there was a fish there it would see a small fly well enough. Mentally you consult the authorities – Falkus and Buller, Spenser and McLaren – but cannot remember what they suggested and in any case it might not be appropriate, so you open the box and pick out something that looks nice.

It is a reasonable way to choose a fly. The one that attracted me at that moment was a size 8 Black Pennell, though I have no idea why it should be so as it was a fly I have since used rarely. However, on it went and out to the swirl of the pool by the tufts of marram on the opposite bank where the small sand cliff looked as though another scour would collapse it into the water. The line swung round and out into the main riffle, the thin white line jiggling over the wavelets, and then suddenly the line took off down to the sea with a terrible explosion of spray.

It was a great struggle, for the fish was fresh and strong and was using the current against me, so that I stood there on the sand like a great dummy, rod up, reel shrieking, full of fear. But the fear passed and the fish tired and came into the sand, fresh silver on a golden beach, and it seemed a shame to kill it, but we wanted food. It made – what? – I forget now, four or five pounds, and it was the size of a grilse so that you had to spread out the tail to be sure. With any decent size fish, spread out the tail and you will see the difference.

sea trout   **salmon**

Dear Arran Island. One day I hope to come back.

A NYMPH IN THE POOL

The general picture of sea trout activities in the areas of
estuaries is that in spring the early fish are on their way
in and kelts on their way out. . . . The best fishing when
there are huge runs of fish present is usually in June,
July, tapering off in August, except in the Shetlands,
where the voes fish best in September.

Charles McLaren, *The Art of Sea Trout Fishing*, 1963

For a young man there is nothing better than to take a rucksack and
a rod and tramp the coastlines of the west of Scotland and the Isles.
I would not like to try it now but in your twenties and thirties there
is nothing finer, and if you are fortunate, as I was once, there will be
adventure.

But to find adventure you must travel light and with the lightest
of tackle, a travelling rod that packs small which you can stick out of
your sack rather than carry, for you will need a stick to walk with,
and there will be nothing much else but a box of flies and some
nylon – no net, no waders, just a good strong pair of walking boots
that will not mind getting wet. For the rest you must be as sparse as
a commando for you will have to live off the country – and what a
beautiful country you will find.

The fishing guides will not tell you where to go, for much of the
fishing, apart from one or two places, is still wild, and only the locals

know of the sea pools and the burns, so you enquire at post offices, hardware stores and inns, exploring as you go; and you must walk the beaches.

To get there you will follow deer tracks through plantations, walk knee-deep through moorland bracken, all the way up through Knapdale, Kintyre, past old Norse ruins, all the way up to Skye, the Cuillins, and beyond, so that you will not do it in a week or a month or a month of Sundays for it will be something you will come back to whenever you can, year after year.

I remember my first journey, finding a little village shop on the sea front near Loch Fyne, asking the man behind the counter, who sold flies as well as groceries, whether there was any sea-trout or trout fishing to be had. He looked at me like an old friend even though I was half his age.

'Go up that road there,' he said, sketching it out on the back of a bill, 'and when you get to the cottages climb the wire to your left and go down through the woods to the sea. There's a good sea pool there which should have fish an hour or so each side of the high tide.'

I thanked him and asked about a permit. He looked surprised. His eyebrows rose.

'There's no permit,' he said. 'There's nothing to pay. If anyone asks who you are, tell them I sent you.'

I thanked him and bought some chocolate and some of his flies, more than I needed, and started up the road towards the woods and the deer forest. You need a map and a compass, a compass certainly, for there will be times when you need them both and without a compass you can easily get lost.

I climbed the wire and found the burn and followed a deer track down towards the sea and came out into a kind of scene that a good stage designer might have imagined for a performance of *A Midsummer Night's Dream*.

There was the sea pool, quite small, I doubt not much more than the size of half a tennis court, surrounded by granite boulders and in between the boulders short green moss and grass and great dancing bouquets of wild flowers all shining and colourful in the sun. The burn fell into the pool from a little waterfall, and you could hear the tinkle of falling water mingling with the crash of waves on the beach beyond.

The colours were quite indescribable and the waters were bluer than the bluest of the sea and there I was in this secret glade that was a kind of Eden, so brilliant and beautiful that I felt almost as though I was trespassing on holy ground.

I went to the edge of the pool and sat on a granite boulder. The granite was full of minute colour. Tiny flowers sprouted from crevices. Below me the water of the pool was so clear you could see the weed on the bottom as if there was no water between us, only a shimmer of light over the weed, yet it must have been quite deep. There was no sign of fish at all but even so I put up my rod and tied on the smallest of small Peter Rosses.

I cast it across the pool, more to see how it looked than anything else, certainly not thinking I was casting to a fish, for there were no fish there. The fly looked good under the shimmer, I don't know how deep it went, maybe a couple of feet, but you could see every detail of the dressing. Suddenly a fish flared up silver out of the weed, took the fly, and shot back again at top speed. If it had not hooked itself I would have lost it because I did nothing at all I was so surprised.

It was only a small trout, about half or three-quarters of a pound, and I hated killing it, but I was fishing for my supper and there was no choice unless I was a vegetarian, which I might well be if I did not like the taste of trout fried in butter. Also there is always a sense of triumph, an age-old feeling that goes back into our bones, inherited from a million years of conditioning. Somewhere in me was a small caveman coming home with his kill.

I was halfway back to the cottage where I was staying when I remembered that I had left my box of flies behind, a small tin box with only half a dozen or so flies in it, but they were not to be lost. Instead of going back through the wood I cut down a track that I guessed would bring me out by the sea so I could walk along the sands.

I didn't know the way and it was further than I thought and I spent some time exploring some ruined stones on a headland which may have been a fort or a castle or a tomb, perhaps even the relics of the Norsemen. They gave a sad impression of a lost world and so I was in a thoughtful mood as I shuffled on through soft sand and round a cliff to come in sight of the pool

A girl was swimming naked in the pool. I retreated regretfully behind the rocks. She did not see me and I did not go back for my fly box. I left it in gratitude for the sight of Aphrodite.

LOCHS AND LOUGHS
AND LOCHANS

Come and visit us. Walk in our magnificent hills and mountains and fish in our trout-filled lochs and lochans. As long as you respect the rights of the riparian owners and hard-working angling clubs and associations, and fish in a fair and sportsmanlike fashion, you will find a warm welcome – always.

Bruce Sandison, *Trout Lochs of Scotland*, 1983.

To hook a salmon on a fly from a boat on a lough is, for me, the ultimate lough angling experience. The power of a fresh run salmon as it storms for freedom towards the farthest shore is best described as hooking the proverbial train going through a station and often you have as much control.

Peter O'Reilly, *Trout and Salmon Loughs of Ireland*, 1987.

It is splendid to have a good day on a loch with good company, a good boatman, and a fair head of fish. There are many where you will get fine brown trout. On Loch Awe in Scotland a brown trout of 39½ pounds was taken in 1886. The official British record was a trout of just over 19 pounds from Loch Quoich, a loch I don't know, which is in Inverness-shire.

In Ireland there have been monster trout, many unrecorded, and each year brown trout of 15 pounds and over are taken, mostly on trolling, some on the mayfly, and all these are wild fish which fight like the devil on the take. There are some fine fish on Sheelin and I always remember when I was fishing there during the mayfly the gillie, a redoubtable old man, warned me not to strike when I saw the rise.

'When a fish rises to your fly,' he said, 'you do not strike at once but say "Up the Republic" and strike then and you will have him.'

Then there are the big lochs and loughs with a way into them from the sea, often by quite a short river, where you will fish for the salmon and sea trout, as for the brown trout, on the drift. My own favourites are Hope in Scotland and Beltra in Ireland but there are other splendid fisheries such as Corrib and Maree where you can take fresh-run sea trout and salmon on a drift from a boat on fine tackle with single-handed rods.

But before you go fishing, remember those things that will give you comfort and safety. The boatmen will take care of many of the items on the following list but you should know what they are all the same.

Do not fish standing up in a boat.
If you have to move, move one at a time.
Have a life-jacket.
A boat should also have flotation bags and an anchor.
Check the outboard motor, the oars, the drogue.
Check that you have
waterproof trousers and coats,
boat cushions,
a big-gaped and long-handled landing net,
a wet sack to put over fish on the floorboards,
a picnic basket with food and drink.

As for the tackle, you know it all: a single-handed trout rod of about nine or ten feet, very light in weight, throwing a light floating line, for you do not cast any distance on the drift, perhaps two or three rod lengths in front of the boat, no more.

For the flies you have a cast – it is still called a cast in most places – with room for a bob fly, a middle dropper, and a point fly. The choice of fly is a matter of serious contemplation. For salmon or sea trout I would have a cast of about eight feet in length with the bob fly fairly close to the end of the line.

The outfit looks something like this:

The easiest way of making up the cast is to take a level stretch of nylon of about 8 or 10 lb breaking strain for salmon and sea trout and then tie in two droppers with a four-turn water knot with the dropper angled up the cast towards the line. The droppers are perhaps four to six inches long and as they are facing up towards the line they make the flies wiggle nicely on the retrieve.

This is the way to tie on droppers.

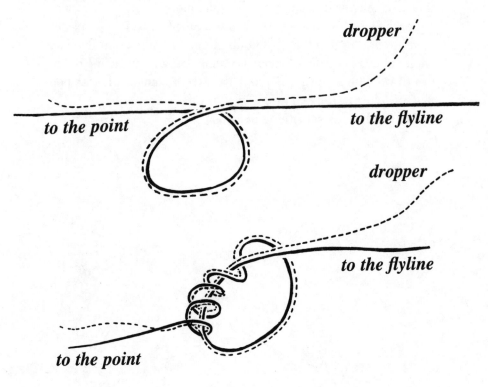

For the big brown trout, especially on the Irish limestone loughs, you do not want to go too fine, a cast of maybe 6 or 7 lb will do nicely.

The point fly should in theory be the heaviest, the middle dropper slightly lighter and of a different colour, and the bob fly a very bushy but not too heavily dressed fly that will bobble nicely over the waves. The choice of fly for salmon and sea trout is up to the boatman, and if he is one who has fished the lough for several years you must leave it to him. The same too for the Scottish lochs.

My own choice might well be, for Irish salmon and sea trout, a Bibio on the point, a Green Peter on the middle, and a Claret Bumble on the bob, all about size 8, but do not on any account overlook the Daddy.

In Scotland you might do worse than a Peter Ross, one of the Mallards or Woodcocks, and a Red Palmer on the bob, but your choice could well be better than mine.

For trout you can go down a couple of pegs or more, and indeed on some of the trout lakes a size 14 Sedge and a size 16 Duck Fly or Blae and Black work wonders. During the mayfly there is no question what you have on: you have on three Mayfly.

I have never found it necessary to grease any of the flies on the drifts. Sometimes they fish on top, sometimes they fish under, but wherever they are you will always see the swirl of a take. The bob fly you bring to the surface yourself by a lift of the rod.

The standard practice is of course for the boatman to be at the oars, one rod in the bow and one in the stern, each casting ahead and retrieving right bang up close to the boat, for a fish can take as close in as a yard or so. Fish have no fear of a drifting boat providing you don't bang about and send vibrations through the water. Go quietly and stay low.

When you stop for lunch and pull into an island or some place like that, always eat with your boatman unless he deliberately goes off by himself. In this kind of an expedition you are equal partners. Beware about drinking whisky midday for you will go to sleep in the afternoon. Wine is as bad. If the boatman in Ireland ever offers you a colourless liquid do be careful, for this is poteen and will go down your throat like thunder and warm the nails in your boots.

As for casting your flies, if there is a good strong breeze, a roll cast is a pleasant and useful change from casting straight ahead for the line will act as a kind of spinnaker and fish the fly for you. This is how it is (see next page).

In diagram A the stern rod has roll-cast to his left. In diagram B the wind is blowing his line across in front of him, dragging the flies across the surface. Both rods can cast like this providing they get the right rhythm.

You will remember that when you have a fish on you must net it on the windward side of the boat otherwise you may well drift over it before you get it into the net and then you will have the fish on

A   **B**

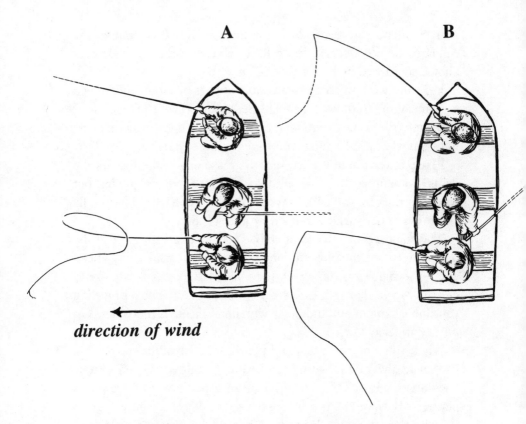

← *direction of wind*

one side of the boat and you will be on the other with the line going underneath.

Whenever I fish the drift I am never certain whether I tighten into a fish or whether the fish tightens into me. The movement is something that happens. One moment the fish is not there, the next it is. If you get a boil in the water as you bring the flies back you must cover that place at once, and several times if it is possible, for the fish will have come to you, missed his strike, and if he sees the flies again may take properly.

Some fishers like the dap. It is a kind of lazy man's dry fly. You use a long rod of about 15 feet – a salmon rod will do – tie on a blowline to your ordinary line, about ten yards or so, and tie a yard of nylon on to the end of the blowline. On this you mount a big dapping fly, a Loch Ordie or a Willie Ross, and you bounce it about on the surface of the waves as you drift over the loch. Some people find it boring but it can bring up big fish. If you see a great head come out of the water to your fly, control your emotions. Do not pull the fly out of its mouth. Wait until the fish turns down.

Now to the lochans.

Lochans are small natural pools anything from the size of a tennis court to a football field, or maybe a little less than a football field, which are found in the uplands of the Scottish Highlands. The qualities of a lochan are that it must be wild, remote, difficult to find, difficult of access, and full of small wild trout.

There is one I know not far north of the Dornoch Firth in a remote part of the Highlands which is maybe a thousand feet up and still overshadowed by mountains. It has a name but it is in the Gaelic and not on any map that I have. You get to it by following the tracks of deer and turn right by an old gnarled stump, up a grassy hill, and at the top of the slope is a huge granite boulder left there in the Ice Age and now full of lichen flowers that scrawl their finger patterns over the stone.

There you rest after a steep climb and look out over hills painted round the horizon like the backcloth from *Siegfried* at Covent Garden. After you have got your breath you pull your way round the boulder and there on the other side is the lochan.

It was a quiet little place, fed by a tiny trickle of a burn on the far side which comes in under a screen of sally willows. There was no sign of man there at all, just a quiet stretch of water bounded by boulders and pebbles all scrawled by lichen flowers that made strange colours and designs. The water was as clear as that of a chalk stream, clearer than most nowadays, so clear that you could see sand and gravel on the bottom, and here and there a sparkle in it as though someone had scattered diamonds among the sand. There was weed, too, though not much of it, and I doubted if there was sufficient cover in such little growths for anything except minnows.

While I was searching the bottom of the pool something from mid-water affected my eyes, an alteration of light about halfway between the bottom and the surface. It might have been merely a change of light, a reflection, but when I adjusted myself to looking at it I found that I was looking at fish.

Those trout were quite remarkable because for one thing you could almost see through them. When they came between you and the diamond glint of the sand and pebbles at the bottom of the pool it seemed that they did not exist except as a kind of light, or conversely the suggestion of a shadow. I watched them for a long time. They were real enough but they appeared to be made of the water in which they moved. Not that they moved very much. They were quiescent, contemplative, thoughtful, entirely self-contained.

A slight movement on my part and they all disappeared. One moment they were there and the next they had gone. I waited for a few moments to see if they would return but the pool was empty. I spent some time eating sandwiches, drinking from my flask, putting up my rod, and after perhaps half an hour had gone there was a slight dimpling of the surface under the sallies. Then there was another, and another. The trout were taking flies of some kind, or perhaps insects dropping from the foliage. Whatever it was, it was something very small and probably much smaller than anything I had in my box. I put on a size 16 Black Gnat and hoped for the best.

The fly fell about right but the nylon looked as thick as a cable as it lay across the surface of the pool. How clumsy it looked. No trout in its senses would come anywhere near such a thing. I waited and did nothing. Gradually the nylon sank and the fly sank with it. I suppose it was no more than an inch or so below the surface when the nylon twitched and moved sharply away.

I had my first trout.

On such occasions I would emphasize that no fisherman should take more than he needs and that his needs should be moderate. The trout in the lochan were hungry, there was not much food, they would have taken almost anything that you were content to give them. I had my breakfast brace in about three or four casts. After that it was necessary to stop fishing. Of course one could have gone on fishing by breaking the hook at the bend, leaving an innocuous shank and the dressing intact, and counting the score by the pulls. I did that once, when I was much younger, on a pond in the Welsh mountains, but I felt a little ashamed of myself afterwards, teasing the trout like that. I said to myself at the time rather curiously that it wasn't cricket.

Instead I lay down by the pool and watched and waited and after a time the trout came back and played aimlessly in the halfway water, pretending to be lights and shadows, and one came up quite close to the place where I was lying and I could have sworn it turned first to one side and then the other to have a look at me with one eye at a time. Eventually the sun went in and I began to get cold.

I tried to fish that particular lochan again but curiously enough I could never find it. The grassy hill was still there but the boulder and the pool were not. I dare say that I lost my way on the hills and confused one hill with another. On the other hand, a dour Scot, not inclined to the whimsy as far as I could tell, explained it solemnly away by saying: 'Maybe it did not like to be visited.'

FAVOURITE FLIES

Dost know this water-fly?

Hamlet

I now prefer to think of 'close imitations' rather than 'exact imitations'.

John Goddard, *Waterside Guide*, 1988

Trout Flies

The list given below is not exhaustive. Many admirable and popular flies such as the Tup's, the Blue Upright and the Red Quill do not appear. But the dressings I give are the flies I have in my boxes, and one simply must limit the numbers somehow.

The Tup's is not far off the Lunn's Particular dressing; the Greenwell and the Beacon Beige cover the Blue Dun, Blue Quill and Blue Upright pretty well; and a Wickham will do at a pinch for a Grannom, minus the green tail.

It is necessary to be rather ruthless – there must be at least a thousand well-known patterns of trout fly. John Roberts, in the introduction to his *New Illustrated Dictionary of Trout Flies*, says that he found something like fifty different dressings of one natural insect, the big mayfly. There must be several hundred of the whole range of olive duns.

Many patterns today are based on or are very similar to the flies that were fished in the Middle Ages. They survive because they are most effective in suggesting trout food. Some I have listed are, however, comparatively recent dressings of the imitative school. Apart from beetle patterns, all trout flies should be thinly dressed.

Many trout flies, generally but not always in larger sizes, also make admirable sea-trout flies. I have tried to give some indication of this where appropriate.

All my flies, including the salmon flies, are tied on barbless hooks.

Beacon Beige

Some fishermen use this all the time for dry-fly work on the chalk streams. It is a Dermot Wilson favourite for almost whatever natural dun is on the water. It should be given a medal or a five-star rating, or some accolade of that kind. The original fly was tied by a member of the Wills family at Dulverton when he was on leave from the Somme in 1917. It was then called the Beige. This was the basis of a fly designed by Peter Deane at the end of World War II, named the Beacon Beige because it was first tied at his home near Culmstock Beacon on the Devon – Somerset border.

> *Hook* 14, 16
> *Whisks* Four or five fibres from a stiff grizzle cock
> hackle
> *Body* Stripped peacock herl from the eye feather
> with well defined rib markings
> *Hackle* Grizzle with a dark-red cock wound through it

May I please warn you, again and again, that an overdressed Beacon Beige is as unpleasant to be with as an overdressed woman.

Black Gnat

This was one of Halford's patterns but it goes back with variations to at least the 16th century, and maybe beyond. You can use it when there is a hatch of midge on a lake, either dry or damp, and it is also effective as a wet fly just under the surface film, or deeper. It is a very small fly but if you want to you can tie it as a size 14 or 12, when it could be something like a Duck Fly.

> *Hook* 16, 18, 20
> *Body* Black silk with head larger than the tail
> *Wings* Small white feather lying well back from the head
> *Hackle* Black

Black Spider

This is one of the simplest of all flies to tie so it is a must for beginners at fly tying. The dressing, brownish rather than black, goes back to the Scottish Borders before the time of the French Revolution and I dare say goes back even further than that. It is an absolute standby in a team of three flies fished upstream wet in the Border and North Country styles. Lake fishermen at Two Lakes, Damerham, Rockbourne and other south of England fisheries find it invaluable as a suggestion of a midge, fished dry, damp or wet. I remember one fisherman saying to me, 'when in doubt, try the Spider.'

> *Hook* 14, 16, 18
> *Body* Black floss silk
> *Hackle* Black cock or hen tied as a ruff at the head.

Blae and Black

I must include this fly otherwise the Scots would get annoyed. It is an ideal midge pattern for lochs and rivers and probably best when fishing the drift.

> *Hook* 12, 14, 16

Whisks A few very short golden pheasant tippets
  Body Black silk ribbed with fine gold wire
  Wing Starling or coot tied fairly low to the body
Hackle A few fibres of black hackle tied ruff or collar,
    whichever you like to call it.

Blue-winged Olive

There are so many dressings of the Blue-Winged Olive that it is simply impossible to decide which is the best, never mind the second best. All kinds of dressings litter the chalk streams, and if there are fifty for the big mayfly there may well be fifty-one for the BWO. Dermot Wilson uses the Beacon Beige, but if I had to choose I would use the shadow BWO tied by J. C. Mottram about eighty years ago.

  Hook 14
Whisks Grey cock
  Body None
Hackle Grey cock palmered from head to tail
  Wings Two grey hackle points set upright

The first time I used the Mottram dressing was during a hatch of BWO on the Test many years ago and it was quite deadly. It is what we call a shadow fly, aimed purely at creating an illusion. (See also Mayfly.)

Butcher

I always thought the Butcher was an imitation of a small fish or a lure until I found a silver-bodied nymph one day at Stafford Moor which was not at all unlike a Butcher to look at. I use a Butcher mostly at point on a cast of three flies for fishing the drift for trout. It is said to have been designed by a butcher, a Mr Dewhurst, about a hundred years ago.

    Hook 10, 12, 14
     Tag Very short scarlet wool
    Body Flat silver tinsel sometimes ribbed with silver
          wire
    Wing Blue mallard
  Hackle Black cock fibres tied beard

Tied with gold tinsel and an orange beard it becomes a Kingfisher Butcher.

Caperer

One of the larger sedges and very popular on the chalk streams, but it also does very nicely on many spate rivers

    Hook 12
    Body Several strands of dark turkey twisted with
          yellow tying silk and with a centre band of two
          swan hackle fibres dyed bright yellow
    Wing Coot or starling dyed brown, or similar
  Hackle A mix of black and red hackle mingled
          together in the tying

Coachman

This is a most useful fly for fishing dry, damp or wet on rivers and lakes and has been adopted by many countries round the world with a number of variants, such as the Royal Coachman, the Lead-winged Coachman, and so on. It is difficult to say what it represents, probably a beetle of some kind.

Its origin is slightly obscure. I like the story that it was invented by Tom Bosworth, coachman to the Prince Regent and later to Queen Victoria, but another fly which was similar if not the same was attributed to a Mr Harding. Anyway, it has lasted 150 years and is as popular as ever simply because it is a pretty good fly and must suggest quite a number of insects.

The dry fly pattern has up-wings, the wet fly sloping.

> *Hook* 12, 14
> *Body* Green peacock herl twisted round the tying silk
> *Wing* Two strips of white swan or goose; one strip may do for the wet fly if preferred
> *Hackle* Medium-red cock dressed as a ruff or collar.

Sizes 10 and 8 are sometimes used for sea trout.

Duck Fly

This is a pattern from Ireland and is one of the best imitations of a midge that I know. It is fished wet, dry or damp. False-cast it to dry rather than using floatant.

> *Hook* 12, 14, 16
> *Body* Black floss thickened at the shoulder
> *Wings* Two light dun or cream hackle points tied backwards and sloping outwards at a slight angle to the hook shank so that they project on either side of the body
> *Hackle* Black cock or rusty brown cock tied as a collar in front of the wings.

The odd name of Duck Fly is said to have come from the fact that ducks like souping up midges from the water surface. Perhaps they do. There are other colours such as the olive midge, the green midge, and so on. Just change the body colour.

Gold-ribbed Hare's Ear

This can be a dry fly, a wet fly, or a nymph, depending on how it is tied. Sometimes it has wings, starling or coot, sloping for a wet fly, upright for a dry. Without wings it can have a ruff hackle, or no hackle at all. When it has no hackle some of the body dubbing is picked out with a needle at the head of the fly to give the impression of legs or the splitting of nymphal skin and the emergence of wings. As an emerger dressing it is fished damp, in the surface film. If you like, you can weight the fly with wire under the dressing, but I don't myself.

However you dress it, the GRHE, as it is known, is a splendid fly. This is the basic dressing:

> *Hook* 12, 14, 16, 18
> *Whisks* A few short hare or rabbit fibres
> *Body* Hare or rabbit fur, thicker at the head,
> tapering to the tail, ribbed with fine gold wire

The hackled fly can have a few turns of dun cock as a ruff

Greenwell's Glory

One of the best known, possibly *the* best known, trout fly, it was designed by James Wright of Sprouston on Tweed for Canon Greenwell of Durham some 150 years ago. It is not at all unlike quite a few other patterns of olive duns, such as Charles Cotton's Blue Dun, and may well have been tied to suggest the large dark olive of spring, though all this is a little uncertain. Most modern dressings have whisks. The original, in the Flyfishers' Club in London, does not have whisks.

> *Hooks* 12, 14, 16, 18
> *Body* Well-waxed yellow tying silk
> *Hackle* Furnace, coch-y-bondhu or plain red tied
> collar
> *Wings* Starling, blackbird or coot

Personally, for the dry fly, I prefer whisks to help support it. Any colour will do.

Hawthorn

This land-bred fly appears in spring when the hawthorn bushes are in flower. It has long trailing back legs which can easily be seen when it is in flight. The hatches vary each year but when it does hatch in large numbers it is such a clumsy flier that many are frequently blown onto the water and struggle a good deal before they drown. The trout are partial to the hawthorn but the fly is only around for a few weeks and then there is none until the following year. There are a number of different patterns that imitate the natural but an ordinary black palmer fly is as good as any.

> *Hook* 10 or 12
> *Body* None
> *Wings* Black cock palmered from the head to the
> bend of the hook with the head hackle rather
> longer than the rest of the body

Houghton Ruby

A spinner pattern of the iron blue which does well on the chalk streams and many other rivers, first tied by William Lunn of Stockbridge.

> *Hook* 14, 16
> *Tying silk* Crimson
> *Tail* Three fibres of a white cock hackle
> *Body* Crimson hackle stalk
> *Wing* Two light-blue hackle points tied spent
> *Hackle* Red cock

Invicta

A highly effective general-purpose wet fly first tied (*c.* 1845) by James Ogden of Cheltenham, used mainly for lake trout and in larger sizes for sea trout.

> *Hook* 6, 8, 10, 12
> *Tail* Golden pheasant crest, upturned
> *Body* Yellow fur ribbed with gold wire
> *Hackle* Light-red cock palmered halfway down the body and held in place by the gold wire.
> *Wing* Hen pheasant
> *Front hackle* Blue jay

Iron Blue

One of the few flies where the natural and the artificial have the same name. They are small dark duns with dark bodies that hatch in most rivers. The artificial is generally fished dry but is sometimes very effective fished wet, when it is very similar to one or two North Country patterns.

> *Hook* 14, usually 16
> *Tying silk* Crimson or scarlet
> *Whisks* White cock fibres, three or four
> *Body* Mole fur dubbed on the silk with three or four turns of the silk exposed at the tail; an alternative is to use pheasant tail herl
> *Wings* Very dark blue coot or blackbird
> *Hackle* Dark blue or dark purple cock

For the wet fly you slope the wings back and it becomes a splendid pattern, similar to the Dark Watchet, the wet fly of the Borders and the north. The spinner pattern is the Houghton Ruby but you can fudge a spinner by parting the wings as far as possible and trimming the hackle so that the fly lies deep in the surface film.

Lunn's Particular

This is a spinner pattern, imitating the dead or dying olive after she has laid her eggs, created by William Lunn of Stockbridge in

1917 for trout that were being 'particular'. See also the Sherry Spinner.

> *Hook* 14
> *Tying silk* Crimson
> *Whisks* Rhode Island red fibres but any red cock will do
> *Body* Hackle stalk from the same bird
> *Hackle* Hackle from the same bird tied ruff or collar
> *Wings* Two cock hackles, palish blue, tied spent

It may be wrong but I generally clip the hackle under the hook in an inverted V so that the fly lies low in the surface film.

March Brown

There are no natural march browns on the chalk streams, which is why the fly does not feature very often in fly-fishing literature and is therefore neglected. It hatches well in many other parts of England, Scotland and Wales; and on the Usk, for example, when the March Brown are up in the spring the trout will hardly look at anything else. Sweet's Tackle Shop in Usk is the place for a good dry-fly pattern. I have found the artificial March Brown, especially the silver-bodied dressing, a fine lake and reservoir fly for bank and drift fishing. In larger sizes it is good for sea trout.

> *Hook* 10, 12, 14
> *Whisks* Brown partridge hackle
> *Body* Light-brown fur ribbed with gold wire
> *Wing* Hen or cock pheasant or woodcock
> *Hackle* Brown partridge, long in the fibre, swept back

For lakes these days I find the silver pattern most effective as a wet fly. Instead of the dubbed body use flat silver tinsel. You can rib it with silver wire if you like to give it more sparkle. The silver body should glint nicely under the brown partridge fibres.

Mayfly

The main big hatch of the large mayfly takes place on the chalk streams at the end of May and the beginning of June and fades out fairly soon after that. The mayfly also hatches on many other rivers but never in such quantities The dun is known as the green drake and the spinner the spent gnat, though why *gnat* no one knows. For the green drake you can hardly do better than the Shadow Mayfly, first designed by J. Arthur Palethorpe of Hungerford in 1950 and developed by Peter Deane. It is a perfect impressionist design.

> *Hook* 10 longshank
> *Whisks* None
> *Hackle* Grizzle or grey cock palmered from eye to
> bend
> *Wings* Two red cock hackle points set forward

A good alternative is the Grey Wulff, which probably suggests the nymph emerging into the dun.

> *Hook* 10 standard length
> *Tail* Short bunch of natural bucktail fibres
> *Body* Grey rabbit fur or grey angora wool bulging
> towards the head
> *Wings* Bucktail tied forward and split into a V shape
> *Hackle* Blue dun cock in front of wings

For the spinner, the spent gnat, I seem to have a fair mixture of dressings, mostly based on Lunn's Shaving Brush.

> *Hook* 10 or 12, both longshank
> *Whisks* Two or three fibres of pheasant tail or similar
> *Body* Thin white wool ribbed with black or brown
> tying silk
> *Wings* Grey hackle points tied forward
> *Hackle* Mostly grey cock mixed with black cock tied
> fairly bushy

Skues's Straddlebug, based on the Irish fly, is impressionist, with fine gold wire holding down a pale dun or ginger cock hackle palmered from eye to bend, no wings, and a raffia body. By the way, do not be depressed if towards the end of the brief mayfly season the trout will not look at your fly. It is not the pattern. It is the fish. They have eaten so many natural flies they are bloated and have had enough.

Orange Partridge

A remarkable fly, one of the great North Country patterns but also highly effective for use as a spinner pattern on the chalk streams. The hackle should not be too long.

> *Hook* 14, 16, 18
> *Body* Orange floss silk or ordinary orange tying silk
> *Hackle* Brown partridge

Pale Watery

The natural fly often hatches in large numbers on the chalk streams, is sometimes taken fiercely and at other times more or less ignored, no one knows why. There are several pale-coloured duns which come under the heading of pale wateries. Sizes vary but they are generally fairly small

> *Hook* 16, 18, 20, 22
> *Whisks* Pale dun cock
> *Body* Pale or cream fur thinly dubbed on yellow silk
> *Wings* Starling
> *Hackle* Pale dun

Pheasant Tail

One cannot help singing the praises of the Pheasant Tail. It is a general pattern which suggests practically all the duns and spinners you find on the water, is invaluable on all rivers and especially on the chalk streams. The tying goes back several hundred years but is said to have been revived in Devon about a hundred years ago.

> *Hook* 12, 14, 16
> *Whisks* Two or three fibres from a cock pheasant tail
> *Body* Similar fibres twisted with the tying silk, ribbed with very fine gold wire
> *Wings* None
> *Hackle* Red cock, sometimes blue dun cock

Poult Bloa

Another great North Country pattern. Poult is chicken or pullet and bloa is a bluey colour. The fly, and the name too, probably date from the Middle Ages.

> *Hook* 14, 16, 18
> *Body* Primrose tying silk
> *Hackle* Originally a slate-blue feather from the underwing of a grouse but any fairly soft blue feather will do

Sedge Fly

There are several hundred sedge or caddis flies, the grannom, grousewing, murrough, and so many more that one can't really keep up with them. The impressionist pattern is the simplest, red cock hackles wound from the eye to the bend, no body, no wings, no ribbing, nothing but the hackle points on the water. It works well as a dry fly during the evening rise, especially when used as a wake fly to imitate the scuttering sedge. For dry and wet fly on lakes and rivers there is a very good conventional dressing which suggests a number of insects.

> *Hook* 10, 12, 14
> *Body* Grey fur
> *Wings* Red, dun or speckled hackle fibres tied in just
> behind the head and splayed out
> wedge-shaped over the shank to the bend
> *Hackle* Red, dun or grizzle cock dressed as a ruff or
> collar in front of the wings

If you do not want to tie a special sedge pattern then a Wickham does wonderfully well fished either dry or wet, especially on lakes.

Sherry Spinner

A William Lunn dressing which suggests the spinner of the blue-winged olive and is wonderful during the evening rise on the chalk streams.

> *Hook* 14, 16
> *Tying silk* Pale orange
> *Whisks* Ginger cock
> *Body* Orange floss ribbed with gold wire
> *Wings* Pale-blue hackle points tied spent
> *Hackle* Red or (preferably) dyed orange cock

Snipe and Purple

Another fine North Country pattern for upstream wet-fly fishing.

> *Hook* 14, 16
> *Body* Purple silk
> *Hackle* Dark snipe

Soldier Palmer

If you want a good bob fly on a team of flies for fishing the drift you cannot do much better than the Soldier Palmer. In bigger sizes on the bob it will bring up sea trout and salmon.

> *Hook* 10, 12
> *Body* Scarlet dubbing the colour of a Guards tunic
> ribbed with gold wire or fine gold flat tinsel
> *Hackle* Bright-red cock palmered from eye to bend
> held down by the wire or tinsel

Spiders

The Black Spider, Dun Spider, Orange Partridge, Poult Bloa, and other standard Border and North Country dressings, are sometimes called spider patterns, derived from a book by W. C. Stewart, *The Practical Angler*, first published in 1857. They are not spiders, more like drowned duns or spinners, and when fished downstream are suggestive of nymphs.

Wickham's Fancy

A very good suggestion of a sedge which came from the chalk streams about a hundred and fifty years ago but is similar to a much older pattern. It does very well as a lake fly, fished wet or damp.

> *Hook* 12, 14, 16
> *Whisks* Ginger hackle fibres
> *Body* Flat gold tinsel ribbed with gold wire
> *Body hackle* Ginger cock palmered from head to bend,
> held down by the gold wire
> *Wings* Starling, upright for the dry fly, laid back
> for the wet
> *Front hackle* Ginger cock

Salmon and Sea Trout Flies

Arndilly Fancy

A good-looking salmon fly, generally tied on a double, which takes its name from its birthplace on the Spey. It can be fished with a floating or a sunk line but cannot be dressed very large – a size 4 double is about the biggest. I have known a fifteen-pounder well taken on a size 10 double.

> *Salmon hook* Double or single, 12 to 4
> *Tag* Silver oval tinsel or wire, sometimes gold
> *Tail* Golden pheasant crest
> *Body* Yellow floss ribbed with silver or gold
> *Wing* Thin layer of dark hair, such as dyed squirrel or stoat's tail
> *Overwing* One jungle cock feather laid flat over the hair
> *Hackle* Rather long light-blue hackle tied as a ruff
> *Eye* Bright scarlet lacquer.

You can leave out the tag and the tail if you like and this simplifies the dressing as much as possible.

Bibio

An Irish lough fly for sea trout and salmon first tied by Major Charles Roberts of the Burrishoole Fishery, Co. Mayo, in the 1950s. In smaller sizes it has been adopted by English reservoir fishermen.

> *Trout hook* 4, 6, 8
> *Body* Black wool with an orange wool band halfway along the shank
> *Hackle* Black cock palmered from head to tail

Black Pennell

A Scottish loch fly first tied by an Inspector of Fisheries for Scotland, H. Cholmondely Pennell, in the 1860s or 1870s. In smaller sizes a useful trout fly.

> *Trout hook* 4, 6, 8
> *Tail* Golden pheasant tippet
> *Body* Black floss ribbed with fine oval silver
> *Hackle* Long-fibred black cock tied as a ruff

Blue Charm

A traditional salmon fly, fairly small, often tied on a double hook, dating back to the mid-1800s. On some of the Tweed beats when the water gets to near summer level they never expect you to fish anything else.

> *Salmon hook* 4 to 10
> *Tail* Golden pheasant crest
> *Tag* Oval silver
> *Body* Black floss ribbed with oval silver
> *Hackle* Light-blue cock tied as a ruff
> *Wing* Brown mottled turkey or similar with strips of barred teal as an overwing, or else mixed hair
> *Topping* Golden pheasant crest meeting the tip of the tail

Bumbles

Irish sea-trout and salmon flies designed by the Irish judge, T. C. Kingsmill Moore, in the 1950s. There are several colours but the one I have found most effective for fishing the drift for sea trout as a bob fly is the Claret Bumble.

Trout hook 4 to 8
    Tail Golden pheasant crest
    Body Claret fur and fine gold ribbing
    Hackle Two cock feathers, one claret, one black,
        palmered down the shank from head to
        tail and held in place by the rib.
  Front hackle Blue jay tied as a ruff

Daddy-longlegs

A sea-trout fly, often used as a trout fly when the daddies are being blown over the water. It brings up salmon and sea trout and can be used as a bob fly on the drift.

Trout hook 6, 8, longshank
    Body Pheasant tail fibres twisted with gold
        wire
    Legs About half a dozen fibres from a cock
        pheasant's tail, knotted in the middle to
        make the knee joints, and tied sloping
        back
   Wings Two pale-blue hackle points tied spent
  Hackle Red cock tied as a ruff

Delphi

Another Irish lough fly for salmon and sea trout, also a very good river fly for sea trout, from the Delphi fishery in Co. Mayo.

Trout hook 6, 8, 10
    Tail Jungle cock
    Body Flat silver foil ribbed with silver wire
  Hackle Black cock palmered all the way down
        from eye to bend, held down by the
        ribbing

If you haven't got jungle cock then you can put in a scarlet wool tail, when it becomes a Zulu.

Dunkeld

A salmon fly from the Dunkeld water of the Tay. Smaller versions are often used by English reservoir fishermen who know a good fly when they see one.

Salmon hook	From size 10 upwards
Tail	Upturned golden pheasant crest to meet wing tip
Body	Flat gold tinsel ribbed with gold wire
Wings	Brown mallard with jungle cock cheeks, or else brown hair
Hackle	A good long ruff of orange cock sloped well back

Garry Dog

A hairwing salmon fly first tied by James Wright of Sprouston on Tweed in the mid-1800s.

Hook	Doubles from 10 up to about 6, or singles up to about 1 or 2
Tail	Golden pheasant crest
Tag	Yellow floss with silver tinsel
Body	Black floss
Rib	Oval silver
Hackle	Dyed blue cock
Wing	Yellow hair mixed with red
Head	Black

Other hairwings with various names – the Willie Gunn and so on – derive from this but are mostly dressed very simply on tubes.

Hairy Mary

A lovely hairwing salmon fly which has several dressings. The usual Scottish pattern has brown hair for the wing, the Irish version has something that looks to me like grey squirrel. My own version is a mix.

Hook	Nothing much larger than a size 1
Tag	Gold tinsel
Tail	Golden pheasant crest, nicely up-curved
Body	Black wool or floss ribbed with gold tinsel
Hackle	A beard hackle of bright blue feather fibre together with a collar hackle (two turns) of badger feather hackle
Wing	Not too thick grey squirrel fur
Topping	Golden pheasant crest curved to meet the tail crest so that the squirrel fur is encased in gold fibres

A nice variation is the Munro Killer, which has mixed hair and a mixed amber and light-blue beard hackle.

MacGregor

I came across this fly by chance, once in Scotland and once in Ireland. I know nothing of its origins. It is fine for both sea trout and grilse on either river or loch. There is something about it of a Mallard and Claret dressing. It has a charming appearance when carefully tied and balanced.

Trout hook	From about 10 singles up to 4 or 6
Tail.	Straight yellow hackle or fibres, not upturned
Body	Rough red fur or wool, well picked out, ribbed by flat gold tinsel
Wing	Black hair tied thinly

> *Hackle* Blue hackle tied as a beard and rather
> long

Peter Ross

Often a trout fly but it was first tied by Peter Ross (1873–1923) of Killin in Perthshire for the sea trout as a variation of the Teal and Red. Very good as a tail fly on the drift.

> *Trout hook* About 8, 6 or 4
> *Whisks* Three or four fibres of golden pheasant
> tippet
> *Body* Abdomen of flat silver tinsel, thorax of
> scarlet fur, both ribbed with fine silver
> wire.
> *Wing* Matching slips of teal tied close to the
> body
> *Hackle* A beard hackle of black cock

Shrimp Fly

A salmon fly which is nothing at all to do with a shrimp, as an Usk Grub is nothing at all to do with a grub. It is probably called a shrimp because the main colour is pinkish-orange. The simplest shrimp fly I ever saw was one tied by the late Dick Levinge using materials which he carried with him in an old Three Castles cigarette tin.

But first an elaborate dressing of a shrimp fly.

> *Salmon hook* Doubles from about 8 up to 1 or 2
> *Tag* Fine oval silver tinsel
> *Tail hackle* Reddish-orange breast feather from a
> golden pheasant breast which should
> reach well past the end of the hook and
> should be splayed to waggle in the water

> *Rear body* Yellow floss veiled with Indian crow
> substitute
> *Front body* Starting with a ruff of white hackle, a
> black floss body should also be veiled
> with Indian crow substitute
> *Rib* Fine oval silver tinsel over the whole
> body
> *Front hackle* Quite a thickish ruff or grizzle cock
> *Head* Black, not scarlet

I much prefer Dick Levinge's very simple dressing.

> *Salmon hook* From 12 double up to about a 6 double
> *Body* Black or blue floss ribbed with gold or
> silver wire
> *Wing* One or two reddish or golden breast
> feathers from a golden pheasant tied in
> flat on top of the hook so that the fibres
> spread out on both sides
> *Hackle* Orange

Thunder and Lightning

A splendid salmon fly, still mostly dressed on a single hook, which
dates from the mid-1800s, first dressed by James Wright of
Sprouston on Tweed who was also, you may remember, respon-
sible for the Greenwell's Glory trout fly. Not all the original
feathers are now available. This is a scaled-down version using the
feathers we can now get.

> *Salmon hook* Mostly singles from about 6 upwards
> *Tag* Two turns of flat gold tinsel followed by a
> couple of turns of yellow floss
> *Tail* Golden pheasant crest
> *Butt* Black ostrich herl
> *Body* Black floss silk ribbed with flat gold tinsel

> *Wings*   Brown mallard or Turkey topped by
> golden pheasant crest which meets the tip
> of the tail
> *Hackle*   Orange feather fibres, rather broad, with
> blue jay or blue guinea fowl in front

If you have any jungle cock, a single feather of jungle cock goes each side of the wing.

Yellow Torrish

Another fine Victorian built-wing salmon fly which has survived because it is highly effective and in the modern version not all that difficult to tie.

> *Salmon hook*   Almost any size single or double
> from 6 upwards
> *Tail*   Upturned golden pheasant crest
> *Tag*   Silver tinsel and yellow silk
> *Butt*   Black ostrich herl
> *Rear body*   Black wool ribbed with silver
> *Front body*   Black ostrich herl ribbed with silver
> *Front body and*   Palmer-tied yellow cock
> *throat hackle*
> *Wing*   Dark turkey tail with side wings of
> grey drake and red, yellow and blue
> swan strips
> *Topping*   Golden pheasant crest